Margaret Pritchard Houston is the Families Pastor at St George's C
With a background in primary school teaching and theatre, she is particularly interested in using liturgy and the arts to help children discover and express their spirituality. She writes regularly for the Diocese of London on children's ministry.

THERE IS
A SEASON

Celebrating the church year with children

Margaret Pritchard Houston

First published in Great Britain in 2013

Society for Promoting Christian Knowledge
36 Causton Street
London SW1P 4ST
www.spckpublishing.co.uk

British Library Cataloguing-in-Publication Data
A catalogue record for this book is available from the British Library

ISBN 978–0–281–06911–8
eBook ISBN 978–0281–06912–5

1 3 5 7 9 10 8 6 4 2

Typeset by Graphicraft Limited, Hong Kong
Printed in Great Britain by Ashford Colour Press

eBook by Graphicraft Limited, Hong Kong

To my mother

That all may come into the dance

Contents

Acknowledgements

A book based on celebrating in Christian community necessarily has its roots in Christian community. There are so many people who have had a hand in creating this book, but mention must be made of a few.

Father Michael Fuller and Father Robert Thompson at St George's Church in Campden Hill gave support, encouragement and enthusiasm as I developed many of the liturgies and activities in this book. And there are many parents and volunteers without whom my ministry would not be possible, particularly Victoria and James O'Neill, Bill James, Mary Townley, Alison Watson, Shy Robson, Becky Barrow, Hilary Brown and Emma Chorley. Minh Tam Janssens is a source of constant cheer and enthusiasm. The children themselves, however, are the primary joy of my work, and their thoughtfulness, creativity, spiritual insight and ability to celebrate with solemnity and joy have been a source of inspiration to me.

Sam Donoghue and Mary Hawes first gave me the opportunity to write about my work, for which I am exceedingly grateful. Thanks are also due to those at SPCK and its affiliates for their thoughtful editing, particularly Steve Gove, Jane Isaac and Tracey Messenger.

Others who have been instrumental in helping create this book include my sister, the Revd Grace Pritchard Burson, my husband Malcolm Houston, whose patience and support sustain me every day, and Catherine Martin, who gets why ritual matters and listens to me chatter about it.

And finally, there are those people who formed my own faith as a child, and who inspired many of the ideas in this book – primarily my mother Gretchen Wolff Pritchard, my father Arnold Pritchard, Susan Bingham, Carol Heath, Don and Myra Ferree, Susan Amussen and Sherrill Ellis.

The hymn 'I Am the Bread of Life' is copyright © 1966, 1970, 1986, 1993, GIA Publications, Inc. and is used with permission. The recipe for Spiced Autumn Punch is copyright © Allrecipes.co.uk.

The story of the Fall in the Christmas liturgy is adapted from the Beulah Land text and is used with permission. The recipes for gingerbread and mince pies are adapted from Julia Hill's on 'Quick Free Recipes' (<www.quickfreerecipes.com>), used with permission.

The arrangement of 'Palms of Victory' in the Epiphany and Ash Wednesday liturgies is copyright © Revels Records 1996. Used with permission.

'Hallelujah' is copyright.

The challah bread recipe given in the Good Friday chapter was originally published in Ann Sayre Wiseman, *Making Things* (Boston, MA: Little Brown, 1973). Used with permission. The recipe for hot cross buns is amended from that at <www.dltk-holidays.com/easter/hotcrossbuns.htm>.

'Lord of the Dance' is copyright © Stainer & Bell Ltd, and is used with permission. 'Veni Creator Spiritus' is copyright the Taizé community, and is used with permission (Music: J. Berthier, © Ateliers et Presses de Taizé, F-71250 Taizé-Communauté).

The interactive re-enactment of the story of the Dry Bones, and certain movements from the dance to 'Lord of the Dance', are taken from Gretchen Wolff Pritchard's pageant for Easter, 'The Lord of Life', found in her book *Risen With Christ* (New Haven, CT: The Sunday Paper, 1988), and are used with permission. The translation of the Easter Sermon of St John Chrysostom is adapted from one by Richard Fabian, Donald Schell and Gretchen Wolff Pritchard, and is also taken from *Risen With Christ*, with permission, as is the extract from the Easter Sermon of St Euthemius the Great.

Introduction

'To everything there is a season, and a time for every purpose under heaven.'

Ecclesiastes 3.1

'We don't have time *to relax! We're too busy* rejoicing*!'*

Marion Pritchard, age six, on hearing a radio broadcast
telling people to have a 'relaxing Easter weekend'

It is one o'clock on a Saturday afternoon in October. The doors of the church are wide open, and a dozen children, some still in football kit from games that morning and some in Halloween costumes, are gathered around tables in the community space. Some of them mix bread dough, others cut out shields and helmets, decorating them with stars, streamers and glitter. A sign on this table quotes Romans 13.12 – 'Let us therefore put aside the works of darkness and put on the armour of light.' By the door there is a child-sized altar, with candles, a cross and a basket. Next to the basket are pieces of paper with hearts on them, and markers – children are invited to write on the pieces of paper the names of people or pets they have loved and who have died. The names will be sung later, as part of our worship together.

After we have performed a set of dramatized Bible stories, culminating in the promise of life after death, and of our place in the communion of saints, we decorate crowns for ourselves and have a snack. The evening finishes with worship – we put on our crowns and take up our shields, one child carries the banner we have made, and the rest hold tealights in holders. The doors to the church open, and we approach the altar, the sacred place. The atmosphere changes. All the storytelling, the drama, the art and the music we have spent the afternoon exploring culminates here, in worship that brings together all our senses and all the imagery associated with the great twin feasts of All Saints and All Souls.

As the darkness of an autumn evening enfolds the church, we are marching, in a series of figures of eight, around the nave. 'Holy Mary, mother of God,' the leader sings, and the children respond, enthusiastically, 'Come, rejoice with us!' As we sing, apostles, martyrs, teachers of the faith, renewers of society and those we love who have gone before us are all called to join our celebration. At the end, we take our tealights and leave them outside the church, shining as a light in the darkness, a witness to the faith of the saints in our broken world. Another congregation, performing a similar celebration, leaves their tealights in the church's cemetery, to remember the dead.

The next day, before the Eucharist, a child asks, 'Are we going to do the "Come, rejoice with us" thing again today?' He is disappointed when I tell him, no, we aren't.

Liturgy is a profound experience, and one to which we should introduce our children from an early age. At its best, it is like good theatre – mixing storytelling, movement, song and symbol in ways that move us, lingering with us long after we have left the sacred space. It should rise, as a good play does, to a cathartic climax, and finish with a meditation on the experience before dismissing us to go back to normal life. There should be a unity of form, with one part leading clearly on to the next, and symbols taking on new and different meanings as the service progresses. It should be clear enough for us to understand its purpose, yet subtle enough to leave us wondering. It should be relevant to our daily lives, yet in touch with the intangible mystery of eternity.

It is a wonder, reading that list, that we ever get it right at all.

And liturgy for children is even more difficult. We are caught between two equally worthy desires – to make worship accessible to our children, and to fill our worship with the great, complex, ancient traditions of our faith. I hope this book will help you walk that tightrope, giving you ideas not just for how to worship with children, but for how to prepare them for those liturgies, and how to give them space and time to process the experience afterwards. But first, I want to tell you what this book is not about.

This book is not about All-Age Eucharists. The services in this book are designed for congregations that are primarily or entirely composed of children and young people. They can be used in many contexts. They can, of course, be used as the main Sunday service, with a Eucharist added in at an appropriate place, but that is not how they were developed. They were developed largely to stand on their own as children's services on festival days, or to be part of larger celebrations with children. They can be done on Sunday morning before or after the main service, or on Saturday afternoon, on Friday night during a church sleepover, or even on weekday evenings. None of them includes a Eucharist, so they can be led entirely by lay people. If you have the flexibility in your building, they can even be done as Sunday School lessons, during the main service but in a separate part of their building (that's how I've done the Easter liturgy – when most of our children were away over Easter, we held this service on Low Sunday, during Sunday School). They can also be done in schools, as assemblies or RE lessons – notes for adapting the liturgies for schools are found at the end of this introduction, and if there are any special notes for particular liturgies, those can be found after the order of service in each chapter.

These liturgies are not designed to take the place of storytelling and teaching. Many of them assume a basic familiarity with the gospel; they are designed to enhance children's understanding, and to provide opportunities for reflection, contemplation and experience.

And this book is not – despite its focus on artistic activities, and on worship outside Sunday mornings – a Messy Church book. (Messy Church, developed by Lucy Moore, is an approach to creating Christian celebration that focuses on art and activity outside the traditional Sunday morning format. You can found out more at <messychurch.org.uk>.) While Messy Church can be a good way of expanding your children's programming beyond Sunday morning, and introducing artistic expression, it is not intended to provide a space for liturgical celebration, and many of its activities are more rigid than those in this book.

Rather, this book is an attempt to make the great feasts of Christianity accessible to children in a way that does not dilute their ability to instil awe, wonder and joy. It is a practical guide, including orders of service, information on resources and ideas for activities, but it also includes discussion on the theological background to each liturgy and notes on encouraging children's spirituality. The ethos is predominantly Anglican, but many of the liturgies have elements drawn from the Catholic and Orthodox churches as well.

HOW TO USE THIS BOOK

The book follows the academic, rather than liturgical, year, beginning in the autumn with Harvest Festival and finishing in the early summer with Pentecost. Each chapter includes the following:

- a liturgy, celebrating a Christian festival, appropriate for primary school children. Each liturgy can be photocopied directly from this book for use as a service sheet. The exception is Epiphany which is more a pageant than a liturgy and needs rehearsal in advance;

- notes on the necessary set-up and preparation for each liturgy;

- notes on how to adapt the liturgy for a school setting;

- extension activities that can be used in a church or school setting. These are divided into 'preparation' activities that can be done before the liturgy and 'processing' activities that can be done afterwards, to help children make sense of the experience. The latter activities are designed to be open-ended and to allow children space to include imagery and feelings from the liturgy;

- extension activities that can be used at home.

THE FORMAT OF THE CELEBRATIONS

The ideal way to celebrate a festival is with a three- or four-hour celebration that begins with activities to prepare children for the liturgy, continues to singing practice to familiarize them with the music, and then reaches its pinnacle with the liturgy itself. Afterwards, the children have another set of activities that help them process the experience. There is usually a choice of activities in each section – three or four stations are manned by volunteers, and each station has a different activity on it. Children can choose which one they'd prefer to take part in. There is also a book corner available.

I call these celebrations 'Family Days' and we have two or three a year. The format is based on celebrations designed by Gretchen Wolff Pritchard, details of which can be found in her books *Risen With Christ* and *Offering the Gospel to Children*. They are often held on the Saturday before the festival itself – however, for Easter, we usually have our Family Day several weeks ahead of time, as many families are away for the holiday. Your scheduling will depend on your parish and its needs.

Here are some alternative formats:

- A three-week series of Sunday School lessons – lesson one being preparation and singing practice, lesson two being the liturgy and some short extension activities, and lesson three being longer extension activities. There are advantages to this method, but it does mean that the experience is spread out over a long period of time – children may not have as vivid a memory of the liturgy a week afterwards as they do immediately following it. Also, the same children may not be present from one week to the next.

- You could use Sunday School time to prepare for the liturgy, then have a lunch break after the service while one volunteer stays behind to prepare the church. After lunch, you hold the liturgy and have a second set of activities, before sending the children home mid-afternoon.

- A week-long holiday club about the Christian year – taking the Family Day model from above and choosing five festivals to study over the course of a week. You can conclude with an art exhibition or drama performance showing to parents the work you've done over the week.

- The Christmas and Epiphany liturgies, and the Ash Wednesday, Good Friday and Easter liturgies could form the basis of a once-weekly Advent or Lenten programme. Each session should begin by recapping what was done the week before, to help children remember, and several weeks should elapse between each liturgy, to allow children to prepare for and process each one separately.

- For how to adapt the liturgy/activity format to schools, see 'Notes for schools' on page 11.

A note on fire

I have been at several services over the years where children's hair has caught fire. I suggest therefore that children under five not be allowed to hold candles, or else that they do so with no more than a 1:1 ratio between children and adults. If you don't want the younger children to feel left out, you can give them flameless candles – a good selection can be found at <www.smartcandle.co.uk>.

A note on food

Many of the activities included in the book, and the Easter liturgy itself, feature celebrations involving food. If you have children with gluten allergies, do make sure you have gluten-free baked goods available for them!

One final note – it would be mentally and physically exhausting, unless you have a large number of volunteers, to use every liturgy and every set of activities in this book. Most medium-sized churches, with a children's worker, might sustain three or four a year. Smaller churches could join together and each host one (see the table below). Larger churches with two or more children's workers could do the whole lot.

Liturgies and church size	
Easy to do with small churches (can be done with one leader and a small number of children, with few resources)	**Harder to do with small churches** (require multiple volunteers, lots of children and more resources)
Harvest	All Saints
Ash Wednesday	Christmas
Good Friday	Epiphany
Easter	Pentecost

Adding a Eucharist

You may notice, as you read the liturgies, how frequently they end with a party of some variety. I found myself, while writing, constantly fighting the urge to include a Eucharist. Very often, the liturgy led to the edge of some kind of climax, and it seemed not only theologically but *artistically* appropriate to use the Eucharist to create that sense of catharsis and completion. However, in order to make it possible for these liturgies to be led either by clergy or laity, and to be accessible even in churches where children do not receive communion, I restrained myself, often substituting a seamless transition from liturgy to party in place of the communal celebration of the Eucharist.

If you do wish to include a Eucharist in these liturgies, it would be more than appropriate. In each chapter, after the liturgy, I have added notes on how a eucharistic celebration could be added.

NOTES ON RESOURCES

Several of the liturgies include room for storytelling, leaving the manner of that storytelling open to you. Others include 'wondering questions' and other elements of Godly Play, while some of the storytelling scripts that are included in the texts of the liturgy are influenced by Beulah Land. For those of you who may not be familiar with these approaches, here's a brief introduction. If you're interested in more theory and pedagogy, I have included a list of a few good books on children's ministry on pages 179–81.

Godly Play

Godly Play (<godlyplay.org.uk>) is influenced by the Montessori style of learning, a child-centred approach that encourages play, self-directed exploration of materials, and open-ended questioning in helping children learn. The most common element of Godly Play that I use in these liturgies is 'wondering questions'. This is a way of encouraging children to reflect on a story by using questions that begin with 'I wonder ...', for example:

'I wonder what the most important part of the story is'
'I wonder how X is feeling'
'I wonder if you could take out anything and still have all the story you need'

and do not have a predetermined correct answer. Children are encouraged to make meaning for themselves out of the story, rather than having the adult decide what 'moral' they should take from it.

In Godly Play, storytelling is usually done using small wooden figures and simply shaped building/ landscape pieces. The figures are kept deliberately simple and featureless, so that the child can project meaning onto them. The storyteller avoids eye contact with the audience, keeping the focus on the figures. The figures are kept available after the storytelling, so children can play with them.

Beulah Land

Beulah Land (<beulahenterprises.org>) is a curriculum based around feltboard storytelling materials, designed to create a visual vocabulary of faith. Using repeated phrases and symbols, children are subtly encouraged to make connections between stories and understand the depth of Christian symbolism.

Stories are told using a script, and pieces are added, moved or taken away during the telling. The variety of imagery used enables children to move beyond the standard 'heart, cross, angel' trinity of Christian images, and to use this broad range of images in their own creative work. The use of these felt pieces is often a springboard for real theological discussion – on one occasion, I overheard two children who were playing with my set of Beulah Land pieces. They had set up Jacob's ladder above Adam and Eve, and across Adam's body was the jail from the Joseph story. 'They're in jail because they've done something wrong,' one child was telling the other. 'But they're climbing to heaven.' In two sentences, this child summed up the human condition from a Christian point of view – the world is fallen and we are trapped by our own sin, but God has given us the tools we need to climb to heaven.

Craft materials and religious artefacts

There are several good sources of craft materials and religious artefacts which I use on a regular basis and refer to regularly throughout the book. They are:

- Hope Education (<hope-education.co.uk>). Their RE and Art sections are excellent.

- Articles of Faith (<www.articlesoffaith.co.uk>). A good source of liturgical materials and Christian objects – good for making sense tables.

- Baker Ross (<www.bakerross.co.uk>). A warehouse of wonderful craft supplies, their website is easy to get lost in!

- Myriad Natural Toys (<myriadonline.co.uk>). Stockist of hard-to-find craft supplies and quality environmentally conscious toys.

NOTES ON DOING SACRED MUSIC WITH CHILDREN

Communal singing is a key part of every religious tradition, and it used to be a large part of daily life. The fact that it has died out almost everywhere except schools and churches means that it's even more important now to pass on the tradition to the next generation. When we sing together hymns that have words with real spiritual depth, we use our bodies and our minds at once to worship God. And, crucially, we do it *together*, as a Christian community.

Live music requires preparation; however, it is very rewarding in that the children learn hymns which then become part of their mental library of music. A child once said to me, during a Sunday School lesson, 'I don't know very many hymns. I know, like, every pop song there is, but I don't know very many hymns.' That is altogether too common, and children's workers should be doing something about it.

He Who Would Valiant Be

He who would valiant be 'gainst all disaster,
Let him in constancy follow the Master.
There's no discouragement shall make him once relent
His first avowed intent to be a pilgrim.

Who so beset him round with dismal stories,
Do but themselves confound – his strength the more is.
No foes shall stay his might, though he with giants fight:
He will make good his right to be a pilgrim.

Since, Lord thou dost defend us with thy Spirit,
We know we at the end shall life inherit.
Then fancies flee away! I'll fear not what men say,
I'll labour night and day to be a pilgrim.

Figure 1 *This five-year-old's illustration of 'He who would valiant be', learned for a half-term in Sunday school, shows a clear understanding of the hymn's lyrics. Note the city in the sky and the rocks in the pilgrim's path*

Having a mental library that includes hymns means that their rich imagery and poetry will be instantly on hand to children throughout their lives. How many times have you found yourself humming what turned out to be *exactly* the hymn you needed to hear, without realizing you were doing it? If we provide our children only with pop music, those will be the songs for which they reach to help them through the hard times of their lives. Now, there's nothing wrong with belting out 'I Will Survive' instead of 'All My Hope on God is Founded' during a teenage break-up, but we do want to ensure that the richness of Christian imagery, and the promises of Christian hope, that are found in hymns are easily on hand to our children as they grow, and repetition is the best way to do that.

Here are some ways to help children become familiar with hymns:

1 Choose a seasonally appropriate hymn every half-term and sing it over and over again in Sunday School. Put up the words on the wall, along with pictures to help early readers remember the words.

2 Have a CD of hymns, some of which the children have learned in Sunday School, playing in the background during activity time (you can have different ones for Advent/Christmas, Ordinary Time, Lent and Easter if you like). One of the greatest moments in my ministry was when I had taught the children 'Lord of the Dance' the term before, and they all started singing along when it came on as part of the background music! That was when I knew they had taken ownership of the song and felt it was theirs.

3 If you can, spend some time before each liturgy teaching some of the music to the children.

4 Choose hymns that have easily learned, repetitive choruses (don't restrict yourself *only* to these hymns, but bear in mind this will make it easier for children to pick them up).

5 Coordinate with clergy to include, in worship, hymns the children are learning or have recently learned in Sunday School. It sounds obvious, but make sure these hymns will be sung at times when children are present, i.e., at the beginning and end of the service, or during All-Age Eucharists. When we had spent six weeks learning 'Here I Am, Lord' and then it was played in church, the children were able to enthusiastically join in – they felt church was *for them*, and they felt included in and prepared for the celebration.

6 If you don't have a children's choir, invite children to prepare songs to present during the service a few times a year, as an irregular, informal children's choir. The communion anthem is a great time for children to perform a rehearsed piece of music – it can be as simple or as complex as you like.

7 Add movements that help to illustrate the words (I've included a sample on pages 10–11) – again, this will help with non-readers and keep children physically engaged in the song.

Good sources of music

Apart from iTunes, which you probably know about already, I have found the following helpful:

Worship Workshop

Worship Workshop's hymn library (<www.worshipworkshop.org.uk/songs-and-hymns>) is comprehensive and easy to navigate. If you have a computer and projector in your Sunday School space, you can use it straight from the website – otherwise, you can download and save the tracks you want to use and print out the sheet music, or just the words, or just the accompaniment. Each hymn has the option of an 'echo track', which you can download to help you teach – it plays two lines, then makes a bell sound, then repeats the same two lines.

Amazon download service

Every hymn in all the liturgies in this book can be found on Amazon. Prices range from 69p to 89p per track. However, I do not guarantee that they will all have the same number of verses or the same words, as I have made several cuts and changes. I suggest using these for teaching rather than as accompaniment during the liturgy.

eMusic

This subscription-only downloading website (<www.emusic.com>) has a wide variety of sacred music, much of it child-friendly. However, unlike iTunes, it charges you monthly, whether or not you download anything. If you download lots of music, it's worthwhile – otherwise, I would suggest making a list of what you want ahead of time, buying one month's subscription, downloading what you want, and then cancelling your subscription.

No organist? No problem!

Kevin Mayhew (<www.kevinmayhew.com>) has a series of ten CDs, including general and seasonal hymns, that provide organ accompaniments, with no vocals, for over 200 hymns. I call these 'hymnal karaoke' and they're very helpful in teaching hymns to children. Often, children feel self-conscious singing a cappella – having a music track backing them up helps make them more confident, as well as keeping them to a regular rhythm and helping them stay (more or less) in tune.

Good types of music for children

Traditional hymns

These have been tried and tested by generations of Christians, and most of the bad ones have been weeded out. Those that remain show an understanding both of the gospel and of the realities of life that has withstood centuries. The richness of imagery, the literary quality of the poetry, and the ability of the gospel to address the problems of our lives will make these hymns rich sources of inspiration for children throughout their lives.

Incidentally, do *not* worry about children, over about the age of seven, 'not getting' archaic language. If you explain the basics of what the hymn is saying, most children with be fine with 'thee' and 'thou', and phrases like 'he will make good his right to be a pilgrim'. Children are not as swayed by novelty as we are – they're used to it. They're used to struggling with texts they don't understand and gradually coming to master them. In all likelihood, if they're drawn to a text, they will be drawn partly to its mystery and to the challenge of figuring out its meaning for themselves. Yes, there will be the odd misunderstanding – a friend of mine dutifully sang 'O camel of God, you take away the seats of the world' for years before realizing what the Agnus Dei was really about – but don't shy away from a good hymn just because you think children won't immediately understand everything about it.

Here are some hymns I've had success with:

He Who Would Valiant Be

The God of Abraham Praise (this actually works with a funky 'stamp, clap' beat added to it, which is a great way of getting the children physically involved)

All Glory, Laud and Honour (first two verses and chorus only, in preparation for Palm Sunday)

Guide Me, O Thou Great Redeemer

All Things Bright and Beautiful

O God, Our Help in Ages Past

Morning Has Broken

My Dancing Day

For All the Saints

Gabriel's Message Does Away

People, Look East

The Friendly Beasts (Jesus our Brother)

And some more recent hymns that I suspect will be future classics:

Here I Am, Lord

Lord of the Dance

One More Step Along the World I Go

African-American spirituals

Many of these hymns evolved in slave society, in which illiteracy was very high. Therefore, they are very friendly for non-readers, with high levels of repetition, call-and-response, etc. Many more recent hymns are wordier, but still very accessible to young people. The constant use of themes such as struggle, liberty from slavery and God's constant love, even in the hard times, speak to children in a very profound way.

Here are some good ones (all of these are available on eMusic):

The Storm is Passing Over

Marching to Zion

Precious Lord Take My Hand

Didn't My Lord Deliver Daniel?

Go, Tell It On the Mountain

We are Climbing Jacob's Ladder

This Little Light of Mine

I've Got Peace Like a River

Wade in the Water

Swing Low, Sweet Chariot

How Great Thou Art

Rock of Ages

Folk music

This is a broad category, including anything from American Appalachian songs (generally descended from Scottish and Irish music, brought to Appalachia by immigrants) to traditional English folk songs with a Christian bent to them. Folk music has enjoyed a tremendous resurgence over the last 50 years, and there are a lot of good recordings out there, which children will enjoy singing along to. Again, much of this music was written for largely illiterate congregations, and so is easily learned by non-readers.

Available on Amazon:

Palms of Victory (featured in several of the liturgies)

Wondrous Love

John Barleycorn (see the Harvest Festival chapter. The Steeleye Span version is most child-friendly)

The Moon Shines Bright, or The Bellman's Song (from the album *To Welcome in the Spring*)

Down in Yon Forest

When the Saints Go Marching In

Shall We Gather at the River?

Available on eMusic:

Every Time I Feel the Spirit (by Wee Worship)

Dem Bones

Taizé/chants/Orthodox music

These can be very good for children, as they are musically simple, repetitive and theologically sound.

Other

Tender Shepherd (from *Peter Pan*)

Hallelujah (by Leonard Cohen)

Peace Is Flowing Like a River

The Finale from *Les Misérables*

Selections from *Joseph and the Amazing Technicolor Dreamcoat*, *Godspell* and *Jesus Christ Superstar*, depending on age of children and the event/season you're preparing for

By the Rivers of Babylon (by The Melodians)

This Little Light of Mine

All God's Critters (by John McCutcheon)

All Night, All Day (by Wee Worship)

Turn, Turn, Turn (by The Byrds, based on Ecclesiastes 3)

Hallelu, Hallelu, Hallelu, Hallelujah (It's fun to have one group of children standing for the 'Hallelujah' bits and another for the 'Praise Ye the Lord' bits)

He is Lord (He is Risen from the Dead and He is Lord) (see Easter liturgy)

Father Abraham

Sample set of movements to accompany a hymn

He who would valiant be 'gainst all disaster,	*Stand with arms raised and flexed, in 'strong man' position.*
Let him in constancy follow the Master.	*Walk in place.*
There's no discouragement shall make him once relent	*Shake finger and make frowning face, as if scolding.*
His first avowed intent to be a pilgrim.	*Stand bravely with hands on hips, à la Superman.*
Who so beset him round with dismal stories,	*Hands still on hips, lean forward, with wrinkled forehead and mean face.*

Do but themselves confound – his strength the more is.	*Strong man position again.*
No foes shall stay his might, though he with giants fight:	*Fight with imaginary sword.*
He will make good his right to be a pilgrim.	*Hands on hips, Superman pose again.*
Since, Lord, thou dost defend us with thy Spirit,	*Raise arms and stand in orans position.*
We know we at the end shall life inherit.	*Hold imaginary crown between your hands, place it on your head.*
Then fancies flee away! I'll fear not what men say,	*Wiggling fingers, push arms away from yourself.*
I'll labour night and day to be a pilgrim.	*Superman pose again.*

Note that the choreography refers to the 'orans' position. This is an ancient prayer position that involves standing with the arms raised on either side of the body and the elbows bent. The palms are turned upwards towards heaven, suggesting that the person is receiving the Holy Spirit, as shown in Figure 2.

NOTES FOR SCHOOLS

The liturgies in this book, and the extended celebrations supporting them, can easily be adapted for a school environment. The liturgy can be done as an assembly (they are usually approximately

Figure 2 *The orans position as depicted in a mural from the Catacomb of Priscilla, Rome*

half an hour long, so a small amount of extra time would be needed – those for Harvest Festival and Pentecost are the shortest), and teachers can choose one or two of the extension activities and turn it into an Art, PSHE or RE lesson, to be done either immediately before or after the assembly itself.

The main problem, of course, is one of numbers. Many of the liturgies involve moving around the church, or time for the children to each write or draw something, which, with more than 100 children, is logistically very difficult.

There are two ways of addressing this. The first is to change the school's schedule so that only one class is doing the liturgy at a time. Since these liturgies are all designed for special occasions, this lends itself very easily to the idea of a themed day – regular lessons are suspended, and teachers plan activities based around the liturgy, with the 'preparation' activities done before their class has their turn, and the 'processing' activities done afterwards.

If you repeat the same schedule at Harvest, Christmas and Easter, for example, teachers and children will soon become used to it, and these day-long celebrations can become a beloved school tradition. You could even introduce a closing worship at the end of the school day, where the classes share what they have done. A sample schedule is shown in the table on page 13 (obviously, your school's schedule may vary wildly – this is just for illustration purposes, to show how it *could* be done). There are many cross-curricular links included in the plan, including Science (bread dough, planting seeds, dyeing Easter eggs, nature walk), Literacy (poetry-writing, persuasive letters), Art/Design and Technology (banner-making, painting flowerpots) and Music (singing).

This particular plan would work with a one-form entry school – in larger schools, two people could lead the liturgy in different places (one in church and one in the hall, perhaps), so two classes could be doing it at once.

You may notice that for Reception and Year 1, time is set aside for free play with spiritual toys. You might set up tables in your classroom with Christian artefacts, as well as playsets that are related to Christianity, e.g. a shepherd and sheep, puzzles of Bible story scenes, the Jesus doll and the priest and bishop dolls from Articles of Faith, Playmobil's Egypt or Rome sets, a doll in a baptism dress with a shell and candle, a Nativity set, a Noah's ark, Playmobil's toy church, whatever biblical storytelling materials you have, and a small table with a chalice and paten, a cross and an icon. Obviously, while many of the year groups are doing the same activities, there will be differentiation by outcome.

The second option is to rewrite the liturgy so that no movement is required, and it can then be done as a standard assembly. Notes on how each liturgy may be amended for a standard assembly format can be found in each chapter.

Another problem, of course, is that the liturgies are designed to be used in *sacred·space*. If you are doing these liturgies in a church, that sense is maintained, but if you are doing them in a school hall or in a classroom, you may struggle to create that feeling of liminal space, of being on the border between two worlds. After all, if the children are surrounded by PE equipment, or are used to eating their lunch here, the feeling of being on holy ground is somewhat diminished.

If this is the case, spend some time preparing the space. Dim the lights and set up an altar at the front, with a cross and candles. Hang banners or mobiles (making these can be a classroom activity). Play contemplative music as the children walk into the space.

Plan for a school-wide Good Friday liturgy day

	Reception	Year 1	Year 2	Year 3	Year 4	Year 5	Year 6
9.00–9.30	Storytelling and wondering	Storytelling and wondering	Storytelling and wondering	Singing	Nature walk – signs of spring. Make notes for stained-glass window design	Singing	Mixing bread dough – set it to rise
9.30–10.00	Free play (spiritual toys)	Singing	Illustrating scenes from the story	Mixing bread dough – set it to rise	Designing stained-glass windows with symbols of Passion and Resurrection	Mixing bread dough – set it to rise	LITURGY
10.00–10.30	Singing	Mixing bread dough – set it to rise	LITURGY	Nature walk – signs of spring. Make notes for stained-glass window design		Letter-writing for Amnesty International	Banner-making
10.30–11.00	Break/snack	LITURGY	Playtime/singing	Playtime	Playtime	Playtime	Playtime
11.00–11.30	Making bread (unleavened – mix and immediately shape with cookie cutters)	Dyeing Easter eggs	Dyeing Easter eggs	Designing stained-glass windows with symbols of Passion and Resurrection	Singing	LITURGY	Writing poetry, inspired by sense tables
11.30–12.00	LITURGY	Free play (spiritual toys)	Mixing bread dough – set it to rise		Mixing bread dough – set it to rise	Banner-making	
12.00–12.30	Lunch and play	Lunch and play	Lunch and play	Shaping bread dough	LITURGY	Lunch and play	Singing
12.30–1.00	Singing, and free play with small group at sense table	Shaping bread dough	Nature walk – signs of spring (finish by coming back to school and drawing them)	Lunch and play	Lunch and play		Lunch and play
1.00–1.30		Free play (spiritual toys)					
1.30–2.00				LITURGY	Shaping bread dough	Shaping bread dough	Letter-writing for Amnesty International
2.00–2.30	Outdoor play, with gardening, one group at a time (planting flowers)	Painting flowerpots and planting seeds	Shaping bread dough	Banner-making	Writing poetry, inspired by sense tables	Writing poetry, inspired by sense tables	Shaping bread dough
2.30–3.00	Closing assembly	Closing assembly	Closing assembly	Closing assembly	Closing assembly	Closing assembly	Closing assembly

For more information on these activities, see the Good Friday chapter (both the 'Extensions' and 'Extensions at home' sections).

There Is a Season (London: SPCK). Copyright © Margaret Pritchard Houston 2013.

Apart from home, schools are the places where children spend most of their time. If liturgy in a church school is done with a sense of obligation or boredom, children will think religion is dull. If it is done with a clear moral, children will think it is preachy and tune it out. If it is done with a cheerful patronizing sentimentality, children will dismiss it as babyish. If it is done joyfully, in community, with attention paid to the real troubles and the real joy of children's lives, if it does not shrink from the richness of Christian imagery in favour of the narrower easy vocabulary of hearts and angels, if it stimulates children's imaginations and points them towards the sacred, then children will embrace it.

DOWNLOADING THE LITURGIES, TEMPLATES AND CALENDARS

Permission is given to download the following, provided that they are not for resale: all the liturgies; the plan on page 13; the templates on pages 38 and 99; the calendars on pages 78–9 and 120–1; the excerpt from the sermon of St Euthemius the Great on page 122; the dance plan on pages 157–8; and the 'Extensions for home' at the end of each chapter. Please visit <**http://www.spckpublishing.co.uk/shop/there-is-a-season**> to download the material. Once downloaded, you will need to enter the password **Wxxy83qzk47rsg** to open the file. Please note that printing is permitted but copying the text or images is not allowed.

Unless a grain of wheat falls ...

INTRODUCTION

The meaning of Harvest Festival has changed dramatically in recent years. The UK is no longer an agrarian society – many children are now unaware of the origins of their food, let alone actively involved in its production. The image of apple-cheeked farming children bearing their sheaves to church is a sight for history books and nostalgic postcards, far from the reality of our parishes' children's work.

Over the last few decades, two causes have come to fill that gap – environmentalism (care for God's creation and the necessity of looking after it, as it is the source of our food) and care for the hungry of the world (sharing our abundant harvest with others). This liturgy addresses those issues, which are unquestionably of concern to Christians. However, it also includes one more theme, less a charitable concern than one of theology – the figure of John Barleycorn.

John Barleycorn is known mostly among modern Pagans, not modern Christians. Among Pagans he is seen as an embodiment of the earth's fertility, her production of food to feed us, and of the sacrificial element of the harvest, in which we cut down the living food so that we may live. But the medieval Englishmen and Englishwomen who sang ballads to John Barleycorn at harvest time, who drank the calorie-rich beer made of 'his' body to see them through the lean winter, saw themselves as Christians. And if they thought about it, they saw in John Barleycorn the reflection of Christ.

It is unfortunate that John Barleycorn is the term used by Alcoholics Anonymous to refer to alcohol – the figure of John Barleycorn in medieval folklore was benevolent and life-giving. Much of the beer drunk was 'small beer', a weak drink that was consumed even by children. Unlike water, it could not carry diseases and was rich in calories. Unlike milk, it would keep. It was a staple of life and would see you through to the spring when all other food had run out. Without the life-giving sacrifice of John Barleycorn, you would die. As the Revd Grace Pritchard Burson wrote, to the medieval mind 'everything, from the salvation of the world to next year's beer, relied on the sacrificial death of someone or something.'[1]

So this liturgy, set squarely in the transitional season between summer's fecundity and winter's death, celebrates the connection between life and death, and tells us of our responsibility to preserve the life of the earth – God's charge to us in creation – and the life of others.

The liturgy begins with repentance. We have not cared for the world as we should. We have not been grateful for the gifts we have been given. We have not shared our abundance with others. Because humanity has sinned, Christ had to die. But here is where the mood changes from atonement to the gradual dawning of hope and joy – because Christ died, because the grain of wheat falls and splits open, there is new life. God is able to bring salvation even out of our sins. This is the basic shape of the liturgy after the litany of repentance (itself based on the Jewish Yom Kippur service, which will be happening at about the same time of year). Some of the sins for which we are atoning are things which children cannot possibly have had a part in – corporate greed, for example. The reason they are in the litany is twofold. First of all, the 'we' in the litany is collective – we are atoning on behalf of humanity as a whole. Second, I want children to know, *before they are adults*, of some of the traps of adulthood. Children know better than adults that it's important not to make money at the expense of people's livelihoods or the health of the planet. The more we can reinforce that message in childhood, the better chance we have of raising adults who don't forget it.

To add a visual aspect to the liturgy of atonement, and reinforce the effects of human sin on the environment, I recommend using photographs of environmental damage, which can be shown during this time. The children could come up and hold them, or they can be projected in the church in some way. They should make clear the damage being done but not be too upsetting. There's a fine line between making children aware of an issue and making them feel scared and powerless – you don't want to cross it.

The liturgy then continues to the feeding of the five thousand (where Jesus is, there is food in abundance – share with others in the trust that we will not starve, and all will be fed), before moving on to the theme of sacrificial death. This section connects the life-giving death of our food with the life-giving death of Jesus. This cycle of death and renewal is echoed in the year. As we are now entering the yearly period of death and destruction, symbolized by Harvest and Halloween, followed by the 'light in darkness' imagery of Christmas and the gradual re-awakening of Lent and Easter, this is a very appropriate time to start looking at the concepts of death and darkness, sacrifice and the natural order.

So the overall structure is as follows:

1 atonement for our failure to care for the earth and share its fruits with others;

2 promise that we will amend our ways, and reassurance that God provides enough and more than enough for us all;

3 acknowledgement of the sacrificial, life-giving death of our food;

4 acknowledgement that this is a reflection of Jesus's life-giving sacrificial death.

The liturgy itself is fairly short, and it should be followed, immediately if at all possible, with the making of food. The recipes I have chosen all involve physically violent behaviours towards the food. We crush and break the food and then we eat it, and we are given life and strength. If at all possible, you should include bread-making – its eucharistic implications are important at Harvest, as it is the bridge between the physical sacrificial death of our food and the spiritual sacrificial death of Jesus. Bread recipes can be found in the Good Friday chapter (see pages 137 and 141) – if you are short on time, use the recipe for unleavened bread. If you have time to leave dough to rise, use the challah recipe.

The liturgy does not include educational material on issues of just distribution of food or care for the environment. It is difficult to do this in a structured liturgy without sounding preachy – if you want to include it in the liturgy itself, you can include a children's address between 'We Plough the Fields and Scatter' and 'John Barleycorn'. Otherwise, use a Sunday School session or a class session before the liturgy to teach about these issues. Some ideas for this can be found in the 'Preparation activities' section of this chapter.

SET-UP AND PREPARATION

1 You will either need a recording of Steeleye Span's version of 'John Barleycorn' or sheet music for it. This version is available for download from Amazon and eMusic. You can, of course, use a

different version if you like – there are lots of them. But, as with many songs from the oral tradition, the lyrics differ from one version to the next. I've chosen the Steeleye Span one because it's one I've used before and it makes the link between sacrificial death and our life pretty clear. Those are the lyrics that appear in the service sheet. You may need to amend the service sheet if you use a different version.

If you have the time and energy, you can teach children to act the song out as it's sung – we did this at several Corpus Christi festivals when I was a child, and another which I've run, and children remember it. Almost a year after acting out the story, a (very cool, trendy, popular) 11-year-old girl in our Sunday School called out 'John Barleycorn!' when we were putting together a list of Christian imagery to use in designing stained-glass windows. There had been no reinforcement of the imagery during that year – she had just remembered her experience of the story from 12 months before.

2 Optional: pictures of environmental damage to be shown during the litany of atonement. These should not be too frightening or apocalyptic. Birds covered in oil, cleared rainforest and a field full of litter should be as bad as you get. These would be effective as a slideshow – if you don't have this technology, someone could hold up the pictures as you go through the litany.

3 A tree with 'promise leaves'. This is the symbol of our forgiveness at the end of the litany of atonement. Make the promise leaves from coloured paper cut in leaf shapes, and write on each leaf a 'promise' that the children can aim to carry out. Ideas: give money to a charity that helps the environment; eat more food produced locally; walk or cycle instead of drive; give food to homeless shelters; buy more food that is Fairtrade. There should be several copies of each promise, so more than one child can have each one. The tree could be made from bare branches stuck into a flowerpot filled with sand. The promise leaves are hung from the branches with string.

4 Food, to go along with the promises – in return for our stewardship of the earth, we receive its goodness. This food should be fresh and natural – slices of apple or home-baked bread are good ones to use.

5 If you are going straight from the liturgy to the making and sharing of food, you will need to set up all your food preparation tables before the liturgy. This includes preheating the oven and setting the clove-studded oranges to bake if you are making the spiced autumn punch.

HARVEST LITURGY

Unless a grain of wheat falls …

As we gather, we bring our offerings of food to the altar, then go to our seats. When the service is ready to begin, the reader goes to the lectern.

Reading

Genesis 1.26–31a

Reader   A reading from the book of Genesis.

Then God said, 'Let us make humankind in our image, after our likeness; and let them have dominion over the fish of the sea, and over the birds of the air, and over the cattle, and over all the earth, and over every creeping thing that creeps upon the earth.'

So God created humankind in his own image, in the image of God he created them; male and female he created them. And God blessed them, and God said to them, 'Be fruitful and multiply, and fill the earth and subdue it; and have dominion over the fish of the sea and over the birds of the air and over every living thing that moves upon the earth.'

And God said, 'Behold, I have given you every plant yielding seed which is upon the face of all the earth, and every tree with seed in its fruit; you shall have them for food. And to every beast of the earth, and to every bird of the air, and to everything that creeps on the earth, everything that has the breath of life, I have given every green plant for food.' And it was so. And God saw everything that he had made, and behold, it was very good.

This is the word of the Lord.

All   **Thanks be to God.**

THE LITANY OF ATONEMENT

The leader joins in the responses, as this is an act of communal atonement, in which we repent for the sins of all humanity against God's earth and God's people.

Leader   Creator God, you made humankind in your image, and gave us the earth to care for.
We have not cared for your creation.
All   **Forgive us, pardon us, allow us to atone.**

Leader   We are too dependent on cars and aeroplanes, and the pollution they put in the air.
All   **Forgive us, pardon us, allow us to atone.**

Leader   We buy things we do not need, not thinking of the cost to the earth.
All   **Forgive us, pardon us, allow us to atone.**

Leader   In our greed for more money, we have hurt your earth and its people.
All   **Forgive us, pardon us, allow us to atone.**

Leader	We do not share what we have with people who do not have enough.
All	**Forgive us, pardon us, allow us to atone.**
Leader	You put your trust in us, and we have failed to be worthy of it.
All	**Forgive us, pardon us, allow us to atone.**
Leader	As we remember God's forgiveness, and the gifts this earth, his beloved creation, has given us, let us promise to renew our protection of his earth and his people.

We come up to the tree and choose a leaf with a promise on it. This is our promise to take better care of the earth. In return for making our promise, we receive food, the riches of the earth that we are promising to care for.

As everyone comes up, chooses a promise and gets their food, we sing.

Hymn

We plough the fields and scatter
The good seed on the land,
But it is fed and watered
By God's almighty hand:
He sends the snow in winter,
The warmth to swell the grain,
The breezes and the sunshine,
And soft, refreshing rain.

Refrain:
All good gifts around us
Are sent from heaven above;
Then thank the Lord,
O thank the Lord,
For all his love.

He only is the maker
Of all things near and far;
He paints the wayside flower,
He lights the evening star;
The winds and waves obey him,
By him the birds are fed;
Much more to us, his children,
He gives our daily bread.

Refrain

We thank thee then, O Father,
For all things bright and good,
The seed time and the harvest,
Our life, our health, our food.
Accept the gifts we offer
For all thy love imparts,
And what thou most desirest,
Our humble, thankful hearts.

Refrain

THE HARVEST CELEBRATION

Reading

John 6.3, 5, 8–13

Reader   A reading from the Gospel according to John.

Jesus went up on the mountain, and there sat down with his disciples.

Lifting up his eyes, then, and seeing that a great crowd of people was coming to him, Jesus said, 'How are we to buy bread, so that these people may eat?'

One of his disciples, Andrew, Simon Peter's brother, said to him, 'There is a lad here who has five barley loaves and two fish; but what are they among so many?' Jesus said, 'Make the people sit down.' Now there was much grass in the place; so the people sat down, in number about five thousand. Jesus then took the loaves, and when he had given thanks, he distributed them to those who were seated; so also the fish, as much as they wanted.

And when they had eaten their fill, he told his disciples, 'Gather up the fragments left over, that nothing may be lost.'

So they gathered them up and filled twelve baskets with fragments from the five barley loaves, left by those who had eaten.

This is the word of the Lord.

All   **Thanks be to God.**

Leader   Raise your hand if any of you have given a name to a toy.

Raise your hand if your parents gave you a name when you were born or adopted.

We give names to things that are important to us.

Long ago, in this country, most people were farmers. The wheat they grew was important to them. They planted the seeds and watched them grow. Then they cut it down, beat it with stones, and baked it into bread and beer, that would help them live through the winter.

The wheat was important to them. Without it, they would die. So they gave it a name – John Barleycorn.

Jesus said, 'Unless a grain of wheat falls into the earth and dies, it remains alone; but if it dies, it bears much fruit.' We will now sing the story of John Barleycorn.

Song

There were three men came from the west
Their fortunes for to tell
And the life of John Barleycorn as well.

They have laid him in three furrows deep
Laid clods upon his head
Then these three men made a solemn vow
John Barleycorn was dead,
John Barleycorn was dead.

They let him lie for a very long time
Till the rain from heaven did fall,

Then little Sir John, he sprang up his head
And he did amaze them all,
He did amaze them all.

They let him stand till the Midsummer Day,
Till he looked both pale and wan,
Then little Sir John he grew a long beard
And he so became a man,
He so became a man.

Chorus:
Fa la la la it's a lovely day
Fa la la lay oh
Fa la la la it's a lovely day
Singing fa la la lay oh.

So they have hired men with the scythes so sharp,
To cut him off at the knee,
And they have rolled him, they've tied him around the waist,
They've served him barbarously,
They have served him barbarously.

Chorus

And they have hired men with the crab-tree sticks
To cut him skin from bone
And the miller he has served him worse than that,
He ground him between two stones,
He ground him between two stones.

Chorus

And they have wheeled him here, and they have wheeled him there,
They've wheeled him to a barn,
And they have served him worse than that,
They've bunged him in a vat,
They've bunged him in a vat.

Chorus

Well they have worked their will on John Barleycorn
But he lived to tell the tale,
For they pour him out of an old brown jug
And they call him home brewed ale,
They call him home brewed ale.

Chorus

Reading

Matthew 26.26–28

Reader   A reading from the Gospel according to Matthew.

Now as they were eating, Jesus took bread, and blessed, and broke it, and gave it to the disciples and said, 'Take, eat; this is my body.'

And he took a cup, and when he had given thanks he gave it to them, saying, 'Drink of it, all of you; for this is my blood of the covenant, which is poured out for many for the forgiveness of sins.'

This is the word of the Lord.

All   **Thanks be to God.**

Leader   Father and Creator of all, we have come together in thanksgiving for this harvest. We thank you for the fruits of the earth, which feed us in abundance.

You have said that those who feed the hungry really feed you. Bless this food that we have gathered, that it may bring comfort to those in need and that through our giving, we may receive your blessings of peace and a generous spirit.

We thank you for the life-giving death of the grain that gives life to our bodies, and the life-giving death of your Son, Jesus, that gives life to our spirit and our soul.

As we go into the world, may we remember that it is your creation. Help us to care for it. Help us to share its bounty with justice.

All   **Amen.**

Leader   And now may the blessing of God the Father, who created the world with all that we need, be with you. And may the blessing of God the Son, the bread of life, be with you. And may the blessing of God the Spirit, who nourishes our souls, be with you, this day and always.

All   **Amen.**

Hymn

I am the Bread of life,
All who come to me shall not hunger,
All who believe in me shall not thirst.
No one can come to me
Unless the Father draws them.

And I will raise them up,
And I will raise them up,
And I will raise them up on the last day.

The bread that I will give
Is my flesh for the life of the world,
And those who eat of this bread,
They shall live for ever,
They shall live for ever.

And I will raise them up,
And I will raise them up,
And I will raise them up on the last day.

And I will raise them up,
And I will raise them up,
And I will raise them up on the last day!

ADDING A EUCHARIST

- Move 'I Am the Bread of Life' to immediately follow the reading from Matthew, and treat it as an offertory hymn. People should bring up their offerings of food to the altar at that point, along with the elements, instead of at the beginning.

- Add the Eucharistic Prayer. I would encourage you to invite the children to stay around the altar after bringing up their gifts, and to use one of the new eucharistic prayers specifically designed for when children are present.[2]

- After the Eucharist, continue with the prayer that begins 'Father of all creation' (found on page 28) – or adapt the blessing from the service as follows:

Father and Creator of all, we have come together in thanksgiving for this harvest. We thank you for the fruits of the earth, which feed us in abundance.

You have said that those who feed the hungry really feed you. Bless this food that we have gathered, that it may bring comfort to those in need and that through our giving, we may receive your blessings of peace and a generous spirit.

We thank you for the life-giving death of the grain that gives life to our bodies, and the life-giving death of your Son, Jesus, that gives life to our spirit and our soul. We thank you for feeding us at your table with his body and blood. May your body, feeding our bodies, make us new and whole.

As we go into the world, may we remember that it is your creation. Help us to care for it. Help us to share its bounty with justice.

- Finish with the blessing and a closing hymn – I recommend 'Come, Ye Thankful People, Come', verses 1 and 4.

ADAPTATIONS FOR SCHOOLS

Most of this liturgy could be easily translated to a very large group, with the exception of the promise tree.

You could amend this by arranging for one or two children (school council representatives would be a good choice for this) from each class to come and choose a leaf on behalf of their class. Then these children could be given a basket of fruit which they would take back and share with their classmates. Apple slices are good, as are raspberries, mangoes and pineapple chunks (if somewhat out of season) because they can be eaten whole – no need to gather up apple cores or orange peel from an entire school.

A small group might prepare a dance for 'John Barleycorn' in advance.

EXTENSION ACTIVITIES

Preparation activities

As the liturgy itself does not include education on the issues surrounding Harvest Festival, a good way to prepare would be to teach children about environmental and food justice issues. Here are some ways to do this:

Food map (Geography/Numeracy/ICT)

This is a good activity for a school. Give each group of children a world map and several items of food, clearly labelled with their country of origin. Using the map, children draw a picture of each item of food on the country it came from. If the country is too small, the picture can go in the nearest ocean, with a line drawn to its country. This reinforces map-reading skills as well as familiarizing children with the locations of many countries, and can provide a springboard for a discussion on food miles and local food.

MapCrow (<www.mapcrow.info>) is a website that can calculate the distance between any two cities in the world. Using MapCrow, children work out the distance each item of food has travelled to get to your city (or the city closest to you). Practise a few MapCrow calculations with the whole group, so they can see which data in the result is what they're looking for, and what to do if the site needs them to select from several cities with the same name.

Each group calculates the total 'food miles' their food has travelled to reach them. Explain that every fuel mile our food has to travel hurts the environment. Encourage them to think of ways they could reduce 'food miles' (e.g. growing your own, buying produce in season).

Carbon footprint

The WWF has a clear, simple tool for calculating your carbon footprint (<http://footprint.wwf.org.uk>). Its results show not just an abstract number but how many worlds we would need if everyone lived the way the person taking the test does (mine is 3.23 worlds … not great. I'm resolving to start a compost heap and eat less meat).

There are some questions children probably won't be able to answer, such as how their home is heated and whether they have loft insulation. You can tell them what answers to give for those questions (use 'gas' and 'yes' to lower their footprint, 'oil' and 'no' to raise it).

This provides a good starting point for discussions on how our actions affect the earth we live on, and what we can do about it.

Traidcraft activities

Personally, I find the issue of food sourcing very difficult. Locally grown food is good because of its reduction of food miles and its support of British farming. However, buying from organic farmers abroad instead of pesticide-reliant British farmers may actually be better for the environment – and buying locally means that Fairtrade farmers in developing countries lose out on your business.

However, children probably won't understand the complexity of this issue, and your goal is to instil the values in them, not to have a debate about which expert environmentalists don't agree. I've reluctantly come to believe that it's all right to instil in children the idea that *both* local and Fairtrade are good things, and not to try to sort out which, if either, is 'better'.

The Traidcraft website (<www.traidcraft.co.uk>) has a great selection of activities and assemblies on Fairtrade that can be used to lead up to a Harvest Festival. Supporting the work of farmers in developing countries and ensuring that the world's harvest supplies food for everyone are just two of the themes that Harvest Festival addresses.

There are resources for all Key Stages, as well as information on how to become a Fairtrade school.

Just Harvest audit

This is a good activity for a school or for a Sunday School group. Introduce the concept of Fairtrade and how it relates to the Harvest Festival and its theme of just use of the harvest. (The Traidcraft website can help you with this.)

Then conduct an audit of your church or school, to see how well you're doing in using fairly traded or locally produced food. The table below shows some areas you can audit.

A Fairtrade audit of your church or school	
Church	**School**
Which of these are Fairtrade or locally produced? 　Tea and coffee after services 　Milk and sugar for tea/coffee 　Biscuits after the service 　Juice for children after the service 　Communion wine	*Which of these are Fairtrade or locally produced?* 　Ingredients in school dinners 　Tea and coffee in the staff room 　Milk and sugar for the staff room
If your church hosts a baby and toddler group, do they use Fairtrade/local products?	*If you serve refreshments at parents' evenings/plays/ concerts, are they Fairtrade/locally produced?*
If your church has home groups/men's or women's groups/Bible study groups, etc., do they use Fairtrade/ local products?	*If your school has a tuck shop, are its products Fairtrade/locally produced?*
How about the refreshments at choir practice?	
What happens to leftover food after events?	*What happens to leftover school dinners?*

Of course, you can also look at things like cleaning products and paper products, but I have kept the focus here on food, to reflect the theme of the harvest.

Growing your own

Many crops take months to produce, requiring planting in spring for harvest in the autumn. But there are exceptions. If you plan ahead, children can harvest their own plants for Harvest Festival – plant them early in September and harvest them in early to mid-October. Schools can connect this with their Science curriculum.

Here are a few good ones:

• radishes

• cress

• rocket

• mustard (if you have space for a massive plant). This is particularly good for churches because when you do the parable of the mustard seed, children will know what you're talking about!

If you have the resources, you could also visit a farm (or an urban farm) and learn about how food is grown or raised there.

Processing activities

I think it is important for your Harvest Festival to conclude with the making and sharing of food. This way, you act out all the imagery you have just received in the liturgy – the violent death of the food, and the new life we receive from it.

Here are some recipes that are easy for children to make, but which will require adult supervision. (Bread recipes are given in the Good Friday chapter.) Make sure the children wash their hands before they start.

A good way of doing this is to have several preparation tables around the edges of your space and tables for eating in the middle. Ensure there's at least one adult at each preparation table. Make the food, bring it all to the central tables, bless it (a blessing is included below, or you can use a different one or write your own), and then eat together.

SPICED AUTUMN PUNCH

Serves 16

I love this, and it's fun to make with children. The amounts don't have to be exact, so children can get a bit messy with the ingredients and it will still turn out fine.

2 oranges	*$1/4$ teaspoon ground nutmeg*
8 whole cloves	*4 tablespoons honey*
1.5 litres apple juice	*3 tablespoons lemon juice*
1 cinnamon stick (or 1 tablespoon ground cinnamon)	*500 ml pineapple juice*

1 Preheat oven to 180° C/gas mark 4. Stud the whole oranges with cloves, and bake for 30 minutes.

2 In a large saucepan, combine the apple juice and cinnamon stick. Bring to the boil, reduce heat to medium and simmer for 5 minutes. Remove from heat and stir in the nutmeg, honey, lemon juice and pineapple juice.

3 Serve hot in a punch bowl with the 2 baked clove-studded oranges floating on top.

APPLE AND BLACKBERRY CRUMBLE

Serves 6–8

This is my grandmother's crumble recipe. The use of autumn fruits makes this a very good Harvest Festival dish, and in chopping the fruits and whizzing the topping in the food processor, we are acting out the violence of the life-giving sacrificial death. Also, it's delicious!

For the filling:	*For the topping:*
4 medium apples	*80 g flour*
250 g blackberries	*100 g butter*
100 g sugar	*75 g brown sugar*
2 tablespoons flour	
$1/2$ teaspoon cinnamon	

1 Preheat the oven to 200° C/gas mark 6.

2 Peel, core and slice the apples so they're about 1 cm thick. Place them in a large bowl with the blackberries. Sprinkle the sugar and cinnamon over them, and the 2 tablespoons of flour.

3 In a food processor, mix the 80 grams of flour with the butter and brown sugar until the mixture is approximately the consistency of breadcrumbs.

4 Place the fruit in a pie dish and gently sprinkle the topping over it in an even layer. Bake for 20–25 minutes.

TZATZIKI

Serves approximately 6–8

Whether you make it or buy it, bread should feature in your Harvest celebrations. This is an easy dish to serve alongside it and goes especially well with pitta bread.

1 small cucumber

1 litre plain Greek-style yoghurt

2 cloves garlic

2 teaspoons lemon juice

A dash of olive oil

1 Decant the yoghurt into a bowl.

2 Chop up the cucumber (peeled or unpeeled, according to preference) into fingernail-sized pieces and stir them in.

3 Crush the garlic (if you don't have a garlic press, you can mash it with the tines of a fork) and add it to the mix, then add the lemon juice and olive oil and stir until blended.

BRUSCHETTA

Another recipe that involves both bread and smashing things. This recipe serves 10 but is easy to multiply or divide.

10 slices of crusty bread

5 tomatoes

20 g fresh basil

Olive oil

Goat's cheese (optional)

1 Toast the bread or grill it until it is light brown. Meanwhile, chop the tomatoes into cubes and shred the basil by hand, or cut with a sharp knife (adults should do this). Meanwhile, children can crumble the goat's cheese into small pieces.

2 As soon as the bread is done, use a pastry brush to cover it with olive oil. Place tomatoes, basil and, if desired, goat's cheese on top of each slice and serve.

Blessing for the food

When all the food has been made and brought to the central table, it can be blessed before it is served. This is also a good blessing for families to use at home.

Leader Father of all creation,
    Author of the sun and the rain, the seedtime and the harvest,
    We bless this food that you have given us,

that earth has born, that human hands have made.
We honour the living things that have died to give us life.
As we eat of their flesh and drink their juice,
may we be renewed and made stronger.
At this crossing of summer and winter, this turning of the seasons,
As light turns to darkness and the days draw in,
may we remember that the fruits of the earth have died to feed us
As your son Jesus Christ has died to save us,
And that in the spring your light will rise again
As John Barleycorn rose again to become life-giving drink,
As Christ rose again with the light of his new life
Which never dies, and which he shares with us
In his body and blood
At your table.
Amen.

OTHER EXTENSION ACTIVITIES

Here are some other ways to follow up the Harvest liturgy.

Making the Eucharist

Some churches may find this idea difficult, but why not have children make the bread and wine for communion?

There are bread recipes – one leavened, one not – in the Good Friday chapter, and my confirmation class have made a delicious grape juice by stamping on grapes (make sure they wash their feet before and after), the results of which were then boiled and strained.

If your congregation is attached to the more familiar wafers and wine, as mine is, my colleague Father Robert Thompson offers an excellent solution. It is traditional in Orthodox churches to pass out 'bread for the journey' at the end of the service, which the priest has previously blessed. We make bread at many of our Family Days, and the priest blesses it at the end of the service the next Sunday. The children then stand by the door of the church and hand it to people as they go out. This way, the children's bread is used as part of our communal worship while still allowing people their familiar experience of communion. As a bonus, children who do not yet receive communion can still receive bread for the journey, the fruits of their labours and a sign of our common life together in Jesus.

Feed my sheep

If you have a shelter nearby that serves meals, you can organize a church group to go and help serve food one day. This is not something that should be done by only one or two adults and a large group of children – in this situation, children need proper supervision to avoid being a burden on the organization they're supposedly helping – so make it a church-wide trip, not just a Sunday School trip.

A different kind of children's sermon

In church on Harvest Sunday, let the children give the sermon. Help them prepare by going over what they've learned about the environment and food justice, and from what happened in your children's liturgy.

First decide on two or three topics, which will be given three to five minutes each: Environment, Food Justice, and Our Children's Liturgy are good ones to start with. Divide the children into groups to work on those topics. Make sure each group has at least one strong reader. Ask them to write about what they learned and produce some visual aids – photographs from the liturgy, drawings of environmental issues, posters, etc. Encourage each group to come up with one 'summing up' point – the most important thing about the environment, the most important part of food justice issues, or their favourite thing from their children's service.

Then ask them to practise reading out what they've written and showing the congregation what they've made. Give feedback and add information if necessary to make their presentations comprehensible. When it's time for the sermon, the groups will go up one at a time and present to the congregation what they've done – one or two strong readers do the reading, while the others display the visual aids. If you have more time to practise, you could arrange for each group to come up with a drama presentation to illustrate their topic, which will allow the non-readers to participate more.

EXTENSIONS FOR HOME

Home is a good place to take the themes of food justice and environmental care, as it's easier to follow through on long-term projects at home than at church. The 'promise leaves' from the liturgy can give you a good starting point.

You can go to a farmers' market and, with your children, talk to the farmers about how they grow their food.

You can also take inspiration from the audit of the church or school in this chapter (p. 26) and apply it to your home. The table below shows one you can start with. Its scope is broader than the previous audit, as this one considers issues both of food justice and creation care. Creation care issues are easier for children to influence at home than in organizations.

A food justice audit for the home	
Food justice	Creation care
Which of the following foods in your house are either locally grown or Fairtrade?	*Which of the following products in your house are made of ecologically friendly materials and/or recycled?*
Tea	Kitchen roll
Coffee	Washing-up liquid
Milk	Tissues
Sugar	Toilet roll
Bananas	*How often do you walk or cycle for journeys less than one mile?*
Apples	
Chicken	Always
Beef	Often
Sausages	Sometimes
Pasta	Never
Biscuits	
Cereal	
Chocolate bars	

Nature-related ideas

If you have a garden, invite your children to get involved with harvesting and preparing your produce. Let them help you prepare the soil for winter and explain the life cycle of the plants, which is a parallel for Jesus' death and resurrection.

Have a special home Harvest meal, with as much of the food as possible either locally produced or grown yourself (tip: homemade toffee apples!).

Make bird feeders – this can be done whether you have a garden or not. Cover twigs or wooden craft sticks (available from most art supply shops) with peanut butter and then coat them in birdseed. Tie string around the top and hang them outside windows or, if you have a garden, in trees.

Make jams and preserves, and use them throughout the winter, to get a feel of what life was like back in the days when food needed to be 'put up' to get through the lean season.

Harvest Home

This can be done with just your family, but it's lovely to make it a community event with several families.

Prepare a dinner using as much British produce as possible. Children can help with the shopping, identifying British-grown produce and looking up recipes that use it. If you have a garden or allotment, you can also use produce grown there.

Before dinner, take some time with the children to make 'shoebox gardens' – a model, in a shoebox, of their ideal garden. Clay can be used to make the grass and soil, while craft sticks, pipe cleaners and other materials can be stuck in the clay to make stems and trunks for flowers and trees. Then, flowers and leaves can be made out of coloured paper and stuck on top. Display the gardens in the dining room as you go in to eat.

Read Genesis 2.8–15, and bless the shoebox gardens, and the meal, using the following prayer:

Creator God, you formed us in your image and placed us in the garden of our innocence. We have not heeded your charge to care for the earth. We have not been faithful stewards of your creation. Forgive us, and help us to amend our ways, that we may live in harmony with all that you have made.

Bless these gardens, that they may be a sign of your love to us, and the abundance of the fruits of the earth, which give us all that we need. Bless the children who have made them, that they may grow in your knowledge and love.

And plant in all of us a spirit of thanksgiving for all that is before us, that we may come to this table in love and gratitude. We ask this in the name of your Son, Jesus Christ, who is the Bread of Life. Amen.

ALL SAINTS/ALL SOULS

Come, rejoice with us!

INTRODUCTION

These twin festivals are usually celebrated separately. A church may have a Eucharist for the feast of All Saints in the morning, and another service later in the day to remember those who have died. (Some churches use this as an opportunity to extend an invitation to anyone who has been bereaved during the past year.) Or it may celebrate All Saints on Sunday and have a midweek service for All Souls. This separation, as though the great saints of yesteryear and our own beloved dead were not part of the same communion, is unnecessary. More than that, as the All Souls service is usually secondary to the All Saints one, it keeps children away from anything that is not wholly triumphant and celebratory about this time of year. It keeps them away from death.

We would all like to pretend that children don't know about death. We would like to pretend that children are not, in fact, innately drawn to stories that have death and darkness in them. But if you look at bestselling literature for children and young people, you will see, in fact, that children are preoccupied with death, dying, and what happens afterwards. The Harry Potter books show children constantly having to face their own mortality and the mortality of those they love. In *The Hunger Games*,[1] Katniss Everdeen willingly faces death to save her sister, and must struggle with the repercussions of discovering her own capacity for doing violence. Even in *Twilight*[2] (which I'm not a fan of), you find the themes of love and death side by side – to love means to risk being hurt, and to face the darkness of ourselves and of those we love.

For children and young people, death, dying, violence, salvation, bravely facing danger to save others, and the question of what we become afterwards (vampires? ghosts? a two-dimensional painting in Dumbledore's office? saints?) are fascinating subjects. If we protect them from having to face such things, we do them more than one disservice. First, we send the message that we ourselves are scared of these subjects. This can be profoundly unsettling to children – they need our reassurance as they wrestle with the darkness of the world. (This does not mean we offer them false reassurances or simplistic platitudes. We can share our own doubts and our own pain. But we must not try to pretend that children don't know about these things or shut them down when they ask about them.) Second, we deny them the opportunity to make meaning out of what they see and hear about death, leaving them with no imaginative framework on which to hang their inevitable experiences of loss, danger and grief, as well as their knowledge of their own mortality.

This is why I think banning Halloween from Christian households is a mistake. Let children play with the images of witches and vampires, ghosts and goblins. Let them dress up as Harry Potter or Voldemort, and then bring them to church to give them the reassurance that all the dark things of the night pass by – what lasts is the morning sunlight of All Saints' Sunday, when we hear the good news that we do not become vampires or ghosts, but rather saints, beloved children of God, with a life greater than our own.

The liturgy and activities in this chapter are designed to address the following themes:

1 the communion of saints – the great heroes and heroines of the Christian faith throughout the centuries;

2 the suffering and struggle of God's people. Sainthood is not easy;

3 the memory of those we love who have died;

4 our own mortality, and the promise of sainthood in God's kingdom.

The liturgy begins with an opportunity to remember those we love who have died – we write their names down on a paper heart and place it in a basket, to be used later in the service.

Then we go into the sacred space and hear stories of three saints of the past: Perpetua, Queen Margaret of Scotland and Martin Luther King, Jr. These saints are played by the children themselves. The saints have been chosen to reflect a diversity of gender, colour, era and ministry – one is a martyr, one a queen and one a social activist. Children with different interests can hopefully identify with at least one of these people. Though not all are formally recognized as saints, they all led exemplary Christian lives, and can be held up as models of holiness and a life spent in service to God, which is certainly in keeping with All Saints' Sunday.

When we have heard these stories – including the difficult parts – we are given candles and then join the saints in a procession in which we call upon the holy men and holy women of the past, and all those we love who have died, to rejoice with us. At the end of the procession, accompanied by a fanfare, we symbolically cross the river of death into the kingdom of God, which is at the chancel of the church. We make crowns for ourselves, joining in the communion of saints. We pray together, and go out into the world to live our lives as God's people.

A note about violence

The battle imagery inherent in the feast of All Saints' Sunday makes some people deeply uncomfortable. But I believe it is important – if we can understand it as a metaphor and not as an exhortation to a real-life crusade.

I remember standing in church five days after George W. Bush was re-elected in 2004. I had volunteered for the Kerry campaign, travelled for hours to and from my nearest swing state several times, and spent 12 hours on election day knocking on doors to get out the vote. In the aftermath of our defeat, I, and my fellow volunteers felt deflated and hopeless. A few days later, I stood in church on All Saints' Sunday and heard the sounds of Ralph Vaughan Williams' wonderful anthem to sainthood. And then we sang:

> You were their rock, their refuge, and their might;
> You, Christ, the hope that put their fears to flight;
> 'Mid gloom and doubt, you were their one true light. Alleluia! Alleluia!

Compare that to the original:

> Thou wast their Rock, their Fortress and their Might;
> Thou, Lord, their Captain in the well-fought fight;
> Thou, in the darkness drear, their one true Light. Alleluia! Alleluia!

The other verses were similarly watered down. Needless to say, the verse that reads,

> And when the strife is fierce, the warfare long,
> Steals on the ear the distant triumph song
> And hearts are brave again, and arms are strong

was cut entirely.

I left church that day shaking in anger. 'We feel like a defeated army,' I told my sister. 'I needed to hear the war imagery. I needed to be given the strength to keep fighting the good fight. I didn't just need to be told "There, there," by a God who dismissed my fears – I needed to be told to keep fighting.'

Most children are able to separate fantasy violence, and metaphor, from real violence, and many child development experts argue that fantasy violence is actually beneficial to children, allowing them to explore the ideas of good and evil, both in the world and in themselves. Bruno Bettelheim argued that fairy-tale violence is crucial for development in that it serves as an allegory for the struggles of our own coming of age.[3] In his excellent book, *Killing Monsters: Why children need fantasy, super heroes, and make-believe violence*, Gerard Jones writes,

> of all the challenges children face, one of the biggest is their own powerlessness. Some children face especially painful challenges: the loss of a parent, abuse, neglect, hostile schoolmates, illness, poverty, neighborhood violence. But even the best protected children, with the most supportive parents, have to wrestle every day with reminders of how small and powerless they are … we need something to drown out the voice in our head that says we can't do it, and answer, 'I can do *anything!*' When reality isn't enough, fantasy comes to the rescue.[4]

He goes on to tell the story of a boy who had been sexually molested by a relative, and who spun elaborate fantasies of being so fast he could run away from anything, so strong he could beat up anyone, before gradually displacing power fantasies onto more distant characters, such as Superman and ninjas. 'The more a child can view the most unpleasant situations in new ways, and the more he can manage to manipulate and dispel his most overwhelming emotions, the stronger he feels.'[5]

If we eliminate all war imagery from the Gospels, we keep our children from accessing a means with which to 'manipulate and dispel [their] most overwhelming emotions'.[6] We teach them that this particular comfort cannot be found in religious faith. We teach them that we, and God, are scared of their power fantasies. We teach them to go elsewhere with their need to work out good and evil, power and weakness – and we drive them straight into the arms of the hyper-macho secular culture. If we embrace the war imagery, we give them Christian role models who have fought the good fight, who were strong and brave. We take that part of them which struggles with feeling powerless, which seeks superheroes on to which to project those feelings and from which to draw strength, and we invite it into church.

As Gretchen Wolff Pritchard wrote:

> [Christians], of all people, should be able to admit that yes, there most certainly are monsters under the bed. You are not imagining them. The world is a scary place. Our life is not merely a journey in which we may sometimes get tired or lost or discouraged; it is a dangerous venture through a war zone, in which we may be attacked, ambushed, or tempted to join the Enemy's side; in which we may be assigned to missions calling for all the courage and intelligence we

can muster. And in that cosmic battle, we have by our side the unlikely superhero from Nazareth, the meek-and-mild carpenter who proved to be stronger than sin, stronger than death; who by his courage and loyalty has faced and defeated the Enemy, and who invites us, and empowers us, to follow him through the darkness to the final victory, with the saints who 'nobly fought of old'.[7]

I have therefore kept the war imagery in this liturgy, and in the surrounding activities. Children are encouraged to 'put on the armour of light', and the original words of 'For All the Saints' are included, complete with winning 'the victor's crown of gold' and 'when the strife is fierce, the warfare long'. If we cut out the warlike imagery of Christianity because we are (however rightly) ashamed of Christianity's violent past, or because we cannot tell the difference between metaphor and reality, we cut our children off from a source of comfort and strength. We need the war imagery. We are God's saints, and we are fighting the good fight. There's no need to be afraid to say that.

SET-UP AND PREPARATION

1 You'll need to choose children to play the different saints. If you would like to include saints other than the ones in this service, you can ask the children to research and write their own scripts, and add them on (this would be a good activity for a school doing this liturgy). It's not necessary for the children to practise in advance, though you can arrange for them to do so if you like. Otherwise you can simply choose three competent readers on the day.

2 Costumes will be needed for the children playing the saints. These can be as simple as one accessory each – a sheet draped over Perpetua to look like Roman robes; a jacket and tie for Martin Luther King, Jr; a crown for Queen Margaret of Scotland.

3 'Heart paper' – pieces of paper cut to the shape of hearts; if you're short of time, you can use the template on page 38. You'll also need markers, and a basket to put the heart papers into.

4 Tealights in holders, and matches, or flameless candles. Since these will be handed out during the service, they should be placed on trays or something similar, in order to make it easy to give them out to a large group of people fairly quickly. The candles will be handed out by the children playing the saints. If they are old enough, they can light them as well; if not, you will need an adult helper to do it.

5 A fire extinguisher, just in case.

6 The font should be full, and there should be a sprig of greenery beside it.

7 Something for the leader of the procession to carry – a banner or statue of the church's patron saint would be perfect, but if you don't have one, you can use a cross or incense.

8 A singer to chant the litany of the saints (you can add your own saints to the ones in the litany, if you like).

9 A recording of a trumpet fanfare, and a way of playing it – the church's sound system, or a portable CD player, or even a live trumpet player if you can. Clarke's 'Trumpet Voluntary' works well.

10 Materials for making crowns – card, decorations, etc. Hope Education has a class pack of crown-making materials available, with pre-cut crowns, sequins, stars and decorations.

The liturgy begins outside the sanctuary, then moves to the font, and, during the litany of the saints, to another location.

The first space should be smaller and plainer than the second – you might move from a chapel to the main church, for example. This procession signifies the journey of our own lives and our crossing from this world to the next. The smaller space is this world – we are joined to the communion of saints by baptism, but it is still small, and separate from the 'heart' of things. With the saints leading us, we move from this world to the kingdom, which is the beautiful space in which we finish our worship. This larger space will ideally be the chancel of your church, with an altar dressed in white.

The liturgy calls for children to be crowned with crowns they have made. You can include the making of crowns in the liturgy itself, by setting up several crown-making stations in the larger space – you may need to clear away some chairs, or communion rails, to allow enough room for the children to make their crowns. If you would prefer to make the crowns in advance, you can – that makes an excellent preparation activity. If this is how you wish to organize it, then the crowns should be placed on the altar before the liturgy begins, so they are waiting for the children as they arrive in 'heaven'.

If your church has a graveyard, you should walk through it during the litany of the saints and pause at the end to place your candles on the graves. The reading from *The Pilgrim's Progress* can then be done at the door to the church and the trumpet fanfare can take you up the aisle and into the chancel for crown-making.

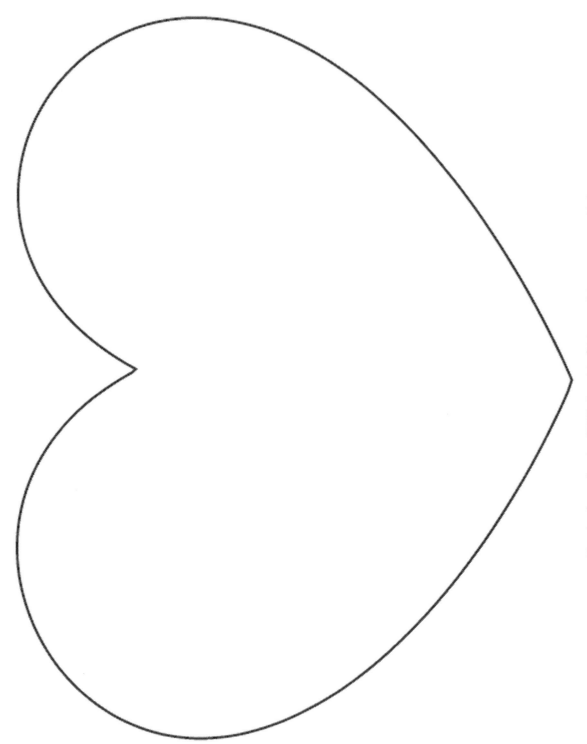

ALL SAINTS' DAY LITURGY

Come, rejoice with us!

As we gather, we write or draw, on the heart paper, the names of people we love who have died, and place the paper in the basket. We will include these names in our worship.

> *We stand outside the sanctuary.*

> *This is the word of the Lord.*

Reading

Genesis 1.1–3

Leader   A reading from the book of Genesis.

In the beginning, God created the heavens and the earth. And the earth was without form and void, and darkness covered the face of the deep. And the Spirit of the Lord moved over the waters.

And the Lord said, 'Let there be light!' And there was light.

This is the word of the Lord

Hymn

During this hymn, we go into the church and gather around the font. The leader brings the basket of names and gives it to the singer.

> For all the saints, who from their labours rest,
> Who Thee by faith before the world confessed,
> Thy Name, O Jesus, be forever blessed.
> Alleluia, Alleluia!

> Thou wast their Rock, their Fortress and their Might;
> Thou, Lord, their Captain in the well-fought fight;
> Thou, in the darkness drear, their one true Light.
> Alleluia, Alleluia!

> O may Thy soldiers, faithful, true and bold,
> Fight as the saints who nobly fought of old,
> And win with them the victor's crown of gold.
> Alleluia, Alleluia!

> And when the strife is fierce, the warfare long,
> Steals on the ear the distant triumph song
> And hearts are brave again, and arms are strong.
> Alleluia, Alleluia!

Leader   Let us hear the stories of those who through the ages have heard the call of God in their hearts, and who have said to him, 'Here I am.'

The children who are playing the saints now come and stand in front of the font.

Perpetua   My name is Perpetua. I live in the city of Carthage, in Africa, 200 years after the birth of my Saviour, Jesus Christ.

Queen Margaret   I am Margaret – I live in Scotland, where I am queen, about a thousand years after the birth of my Saviour, Jesus Christ.

Martin Luther King, Jr   My name is the Reverend Doctor Martin Luther King, Jr. I live in America, and I was born in 1929.

Perpetua   My congregation must worship in secret, for Carthage is under control of Rome, where it is illegal to be a Christian. My servant, Felicity, and I have been arrested for being Christians, and we are in prison. My child, my dear child, has been taken from me. The prison is filthy. Those around me are ill. They look to me to be their leader, as I was in our church, instructing them on the word of God, preaching the good news to them. I seek to comfort them in their sorrow, reminding them that Christ suffered as we do.

Queen Margaret   My husband is King Malcolm the Third of Scotland. Ever since I was a child, I have felt the presence of God close to me, and now that I am queen, I know I may shape this country to be more like the kingdom of God. I have given money for the building of churches, and for boats to carry pilgrims to places where they may pray and worship God. When a young peasant woman gave me her baby to bless, I slipped gold coins in among its blankets, for I believe that God does not wish for anyone to go hungry.

Martin Luther King, Jr   My ancestors were brought to America as slaves. Almost a hundred years ago, slavery ended in America, but there is still racism and prejudice. Black people and white people are not allowed to attend the same schools, or go to the same restaurants. Now I am leading a movement to end prejudice in America. When the police attack us, we do not fight back. When we are arrested, we do not fight back. Jesus told us to love our enemies, and to turn the other cheek.

This is from a famous speech I gave in 1963:

I say to you today, my friends, even though we face the difficulties of today and tomorrow, I still have a dream. I have a dream that one day this nation will rise up and live out the true meaning of its creed – 'We hold these truths to be self-evident that all men are created equal.'

I have a dream that one day on the red hills of Georgia the sons of former slaves and the sons of former slave-owners will be able to sit down together at the table of brotherhood.

I have a dream today.

Leader   Perpetua was killed in the gladiatorial arena, in the year 203. *(Perpetua returns to her seat.)*

Queen Margaret died in 1093, but one of the caves where she prayed can still be visited today. *(Queen Margaret returns to her seat.)*

Martin Luther King, Jr was shot dead in 1968, at the age of 39. His speeches calling for justice and healing between people of different races are still read widely today. *(Martin Luther King, Jr returns to his seat.)*

God calls us to follow the example of his saints, to live lives that are close to God. Let us praise God in song, promising to follow him when he calls to us, and receive the light of his presence.

Hymn

During this hymn, the saints go around and hand out candles.

> He who would valiant be 'gainst all disaster,
> Let him in constancy follow the Master.
> There's no discouragement shall make him once relent
> His first avowed intent to be a pilgrim.
>
> Who so beset him round with dismal stories
> Do but themselves confound – his strength the more is.
> No foes shall stay his might; though he with giants fight,
> He will make good his right to be a pilgrim.
>
> Since, Lord, Thou dost defend us with Thy Spirit,
> We know we at the end, shall life inherit.
> Then fancies flee away! I'll fear not what men say,
> I'll labour night and day to be a pilgrim.

Leader   The night is far gone, the day is at hand. Let us therefore cast aside the works of darkness and put on the armour of light! Do you renounce evil?

All   **I renounce evil!**

Leader   Do you turn to Christ?

All   **I turn to Christ!**

The leader sprinkles us all with water to remind us of our baptism.

Leader   The Spirit of the Lord is like water in the desert. In the water of your baptism, you died with Christ and were born again to his new life. Let us walk in the path the saints have walked before us, dying and rising again with Jesus.

The leader tells us that we are going to march around the church in a procession with our candles. The singer leads the procession, holding the papers with names from the basket.

Leader: Holy Mary, mother of God

All: Come, rejoice with us!

(Using the same pattern, the singer calls on the following groups of saints. We respond as we process around the church, 'Come, rejoice with us!')

Singer   Abraham and | Sarah:
All   **Come, rejoice with us!**

Singer   Moses and E- | lijah:
All   **Come, rejoice with us!**

Singer   Miriam and | Esther:
All   **Come, rejoice with us!**

Singer   John the Baptist, Simeon and | Anna:
All   **Come, rejoice with us!**

Singer   ALL YOU HOLY PEOPLE OF | ISRAEL:
All   **Come, rejoice with us!**

Singer   Peter, Paul and | James:
All   **Come, rejoice with us!**

Singer   Lazarus, Mary and | Martha:
All   **Come, rejoice with us!**

Singer   Doubting Thomas, Mary | Magdalene:
All   **Come, rejoice with us!**

Singer   ALL YOU HOLY A- | POSTLES:
All   **Come, rejoice with us!**

Singer   Stephen, Polycarp and Per- | petua:
All   **Come, rejoice with us!**

Singer   Thomas More, William | Tyndale:
All   **Come, rejoice with us!**

Singer   Martin Luther King, Oscar Ro- | mero:
All   **Come, rejoice with us!**

Singer   ALL YOU HOLY | MARTYRS:
All   **Come, rejoice with us!**

Singer   Matthew, Mark, Luke and | John:
All   **Come, rejoice with us!**

Singer   Patrick and Co- | lumba:
All   **Come, rejoice with us!**

Singer   C. S. | Lewis:
All   **Come, rejoice with us!**

Singer   ALL YOU HOLY EVANGELISTS, PASTORS AND | TEACHERS:
All   **Come, rejoice with us!**

Singer   John Bunyan, John Milton, William | Shakespeare:
All   **Come, rejoice with us!**

Singer   Elizabeth Gaskell, William | Morris:
All   **Come, rejoice with us!**

Singer   Sydney Carter, Ralph Vaughan | Williams:
All   **Come, rejoice with us!**

Singer   ALL YOU HOLY WRITERS, ARTISTS AND PER- | FORMERS:
All   **Come, rejoice with us!**

Singer   Florence Nightingale, Mary | Seacole:
All   **Come, rejoice with us!**

Singer   William Wilberforce, Thomas | Clarkson:
All   **Come, rejoice with us!**

Singer   ALL YOU HOLY RENEWERS OF SO- | CIETY:
All   **Come, rejoice with us!**

(The singer reads out the names from the basket.)

Singer   ALL THOSE WE LOVE WHO HAVE GONE BE- | FORE US:
All   **Come, rejoice with us!**

Singer   O ALL YOU HOLY SAINTS TO- | GETHER:
All   **Come, rejoice with us!**

(We pause at the entrance to the new space.)

Leader   The saints are men and women, as we are. They are old and young, as we are, rich and poor, as we are. They are black and white and every colour in between, as we are. And they lived, as we do. And like they have, one day, we will all die.

We blow out our candles and place them as the leader asks us to do.

Reading

From *The Pilgrim's Progress* by John Bunyan

Reader   Then Valiant-for-Truth said, 'I am going to my Father's; and though with great difficulty I have got here, yet now I do not repent me of all the trouble I have been at to arrive where I am. My sword I give to him that shall succeed me in my pilgrimage, and my courage and skill to him that can get it. My marks and scars I carry with me, to be a witness for me that I have fought His battles who will now be my rewarder.'

     When the day had come, many accompanied him to the river-side, into which as he went, he said, 'Death, where is thy sting?' And as he went down deeper, he said, 'Grave, where is thy victory?'

     So he passed over, and all the trumpets sounded for him on the other side.

We pass into the new space, which is beautifully decorated, as trumpet music plays for us. If we have not made crowns already, we make them now. If we have already made crowns, the crowns are on the altar – we find ours and put it on. (When everyone has made and/or is wearing a crown, we gather in a circle around the altar.)

Reading

Revelation 7.9–10, 13–14, 16–17

Reader   A reading from the book of Revelation.

After this I looked, and behold, a great multitude which no man could number, from every nation, from all tribes and peoples and tongues, standing before the throne and before the Lamb, clothed in white robes, with palm branches in their hands, and crying out with a loud voice, 'Salvation belongs to our God who sits upon the throne, and to the Lamb!

Then one of the elders addressed me, saying, 'Who are these, clothed in white robes, and where have they come from?' I said to him, 'Sir, you know.'

And he said to me, 'These are they who have come out of the great tribulation; they have washed their robes and made them white in the blood of the Lamb.

'They shall hunger no more, neither thirst any more; the sun shall not strike them, nor any scorching heat. For the Lamb in the midst of the throne will be their shepherd, and he will guide them to springs of living water; and God will wipe away every tear from their eyes.'

This is the word of the Lord.

All   **Thanks be to God.**

Leader   Let us join with the saints of God, that great cloud of witnesses, and pray to the Lord.
In thanksgiving for all the blessings we have received, let us pray to the Lord.
All   **Lord, hear our prayer.**

Leader   For our church, our community, as we try to live as Jesus wanted, to be the communion of saints, let us pray to the Lord.
All   **Lord, hear our prayer.**

Leader   For anything in our lives that is causing us to be worried, or scared, or sad, let us pray to the Lord.
All   **Lord, hear our prayer.**

Leader   For our families and friends, for anyone we know who is having a problem in their lives, who is being treated unfairly, or who is ill, let us pray to the Lord.
All   **Lord, hear our prayer.**

Leader   For our country, that our leaders may make the right decisions, let us pray to the Lord.
All   **Lord, hear our prayer.**

Leader   For everyone who does not have enough to eat, or does not have a safe place to live. For people who do not have jobs, or who are homeless, let us pray to the Lord.
All   **Lord, hear our prayer.**

Leader   For people who live in places where there are wars or violence, that God may help bring peace to the whole world, and that they shall beat their swords into ploughshares and make war no more, let us pray to the Lord.
All   **Lord, hear our prayer.**

Leader   For all who have died – people we love, pets we love, or people we do not know. That they may have a place in your kingdom, where there is no more sadness or crying or death, and where you wipe away every tear from our eyes, let us pray to the Lord.

All   **Lord, hear our prayer.**

Leader   And we pray for ourselves, that we may know your love in our hearts, do your work in the world, and, at the end of our lives, join with all your saints in glory, to praise your name for ever. Let us pray to the Lord.

All   **Amen!**

Hymn

Leader   Go forth, as saints of God, rejoicing in his love!

All   **Amen!**

ADDING A EUCHARIST

This is one of the easiest services to add a Eucharist to. When everyone has finished making their crowns and/or put them on, gather the group around the altar and do it then. You may wish to cut the prayers, in that case, as to have intercessions immediately following a Eucharist is a bit odd, theologically – going from celebration to petition, rather than the other way round – and it would also make the liturgy quite long.

ADAPTATIONS FOR SCHOOLS

There are two challenges when doing this liturgy with a larger group. The first is the crown-making, so I would suggest that you organize the children to make crowns beforehand, placing them on the altar for them to be put on during the liturgy, as mentioned in the 'Set-up and preparation' section.

The other challenge is the transition from the first space to the second. This sense of movement from one place to another is crucial to the message of the liturgy – that we are on a journey, from earth to heaven. The second space should therefore be warmer and homelier, more beautifully decorated or more majestic, than the first.

If you have two halls, you can use one as the first space and the other as the second, keeping one plain and decorating the other. Alternatively, you could start the liturgy outside and come inside to the hall, though in October or November this means you're taking your chances with the weather. If you have access to a church, you can start the liturgy in the school hall and move to the church.

You will be moving as you sing the litany of the saints. It is very difficult to get a long line of people to sing all together, so in order to make this easier, I recommend the following:

1 Organize the children so they walk two by two, instead of in single file, to shorten the line.

2 Stop at certain places along the route between the first space and the second, to allow the back of the line time to catch up. This includes any doors, before turns in corridors, etc.

3 You can divide the leading of the litany of the saints among several people, who are stationed at different places along the line. The first person, at the front, can sing the first line, the second one the second line, and so on. This way, children in the middle and at the back won't always be straining to hear what's being sung at the front.

4 If you have a complex route, you can pause the liturgy, choose a place to meet, move the children to that point one class at a time, and then pick up the liturgy where you left off. For example, you can reach the point where you begin the litany of the saints, and announce that you will continue this outside. Stress that you expect the children to be absolutely quiet, and dismiss one class at a time to line up on the playground, at the gate of the road that leads to the church. When you get there, hand out the banner (or banners, if you have made more than one and if you are using them – see 'Set-up and preparation', page 36), get the procession leader in place, and say, 'We will now continue our worship with the litany of the saints. Your response is "Come, rejoice with us".' Then begin the procession to the church.

EXTENSION ACTIVITIES

Preparation activities

Procession banners

Banners have a variety of liturgical purposes. They can be carried in procession or hung in the church. Children enjoy seeing their work used in church services or on display in the sanctuary, and making a variety of banners that can be rotated with the liturgical seasons is a good way of including their work.

A very good way to prepare children for this service would be for them to research the lives of some of the saints mentioned in the litany of the saints. They could then make banners depicting the saint and something to do with the saint's life (e.g. John Milton could be shown with a pen, Florence Nightingale with a lamp, etc.). These banners could then be carried in the opening procession of the service and during the litany of the saints.

This will enable children to gain some background knowledge of the lives of saints before the liturgy, which means they will get more out of the experience than if they came to it cold. They will also probably be listening out for 'their' saint during the litany of the saints, which will give them a feeling of ownership and capture their attention.

Until your children are experienced banner-makers, this activity requires some adult oversight. Left to their own devices, children will make a banner that lacks overall coherence and, more importantly, bits of it will be upside-down or sideways, based on where the children were standing when the banner was made. This does not mean that you direct the children's thoughts. Instead, you provide inspiration and organization. Start by helping the children decide which saint they want the banner to show. Then, help them make a mental (or physical) list of everything they want to include, and help them decide on who's going to do which part.

For the background, I've found that shiny fabrics look very luxurious and festive, but they show every stray bit of glue, while plain coloured cotton is much more forgiving. The banner decorations can be made using felt, which doesn't fray, so it can be cut and glued directly onto the background using ordinary PVA glue.

Banners can be made in two ways, depending on how you want to carry them. The first way is easier, but it is limiting in how it can be used – the banner is wide but not very high (ours are approximately 1 m high and 1.5 m wide), hemmed on all four sides, and is carried in front of several people at the head of a procession. It's suitable for making banners that will be carried outside, for Palm Sunday and Easter (see Figure 3), but not so useful for processing up an aisle!

The other way (see Figure 4) is more labour-intensive, but creates a more elegant result. With this method, the banner is made tall and narrow (approximately 1 m high and 0.5 m wide), and about 10 cm is left blank at the top. This part is turned over to create a pocket through which a dowel can go. A semicircular hole is now cut in the middle. On either side of the dowel, and also in its middle, sticking up through the semicircular hole, you screw in eye hooks. You then tie a ribbon to the two eye hooks at the ends of the dowel.

Finally, you take a second dowel. Screw cup hooks into it in two places – the distance between the two cup hooks should be the same as that between the top of the ribbon and the eye hook in the middle of your first dowel. You then hook one cup hook around the ribbon and the second into the eye hook, and a child can hold the second dowel, carrying the banner ahead of him or her.

Figure 3 *A Palm Sunday banner*

Keep supervising to remind the children which part of the banner is the top, so the picture comes out right side up! You may want to add some cut-out letters to create text that helps explain what the banner shows. When some children in one of my programmes decided that their creation banner was going to be made of large abstract shapes in a variety of colours, and explained to me that this was the first day of creation, I cut out the words 'Let There Be Light!' and fitted them in around their design. It is important to ask the children's permission before doing this, of course.

The armour of light

This idea came from the Spiritual Child Network (<spiritualchild.co.uk>) – I added some of the details, but the inspiration is from them. Set up a table with black card on it and templates for shields (you can find a great variety just by Googling 'shield template'). Children can make their own shields and decorate them – all the decorations should be *light*, covering up the blackness of the shield with the imagery of light. You can use coloured streamers, gold stars, sequins, coloured ribbon, coloured foil, etc. I suggest putting up a sign by the table with 'The night is far gone, the day is at hand. Let us then cast off the works of darkness and put on the armour of light. – Romans 13.12' written on it. Children can then wear their shields into the service – by the end of the service they will be wearing their crowns and carrying their shields, symbolizing the struggles of the lives of the saints and their crown of glory in heaven.

Headstone-rubbing

If your church has a graveyard, you can send children out with A3 paper and crayons, and they can make rubbings from the headstones. When you come back in, you can make a list of images and phrases you found on the graves, e.g. angels, skulls, crosses. You can add the names from your church's graves to the litany of the saints, connecting your church community to its past.

Figure 4 *A banner depicting St George*

If you don't have a graveyard, your church probably has some memorials on the walls
(a war memorial, if nothing else) and you can make rubbings of these instead.

Pew ends

Using coloured card, children can make models of saints they have learned about. They can then fill
in a card with the saint's name, their own name, and a short biography of the saint. Using Blu-Tack,
you can attach these to the ends of your pews, so that on All Saints' Sunday, each pew has its own
'patron saint'.

Alternatively, the children could make puppets of saints to take home instead. Baker Ross and
Hope Education both sell cotton hand puppets that can be decorated with felt or fabric markers.

Processing activities

Saint T-shirts

Buy lots of white T-shirts in different sizes (available in the school uniform sections of high street clothing stores) and some fabric pens. Children can make T-shirts with 'Saint [their name]' on them, and pictures of themselves as saints. Some older children will probably be embarrassed by this, so you can allow them to make T-shirts of historical saints, or make ones for younger siblings.

The communion of saints

The Eucharist is how we symbolize the fact that we are the communion of saints, united as one in Christ's body. You can make bread (see the Good Friday chapter for a bread sculpture recipe and examples of sculptures) or you can have a bread tasting table available.

Use bread from different cultures (Italian breadsticks, Indian naan, matzoh from the Jewish tradition, tortillas from Spain, etc.) and explain to children that in the Eucharist, we are united with Christians from all over the world. Make sure you include gluten-free bread for children who may have gluten allergies. For an extra treat, put out Nutella, jam, etc.

EXTENSIONS FOR HOME

The activities for home surrounding All Saints/All Souls are designed to take the concepts of sainthood and remembering the dead and make them personal. In the liturgy we have celebrated the fact that together, we are the communion of saints – at home, we remember our individual life stories, the saints that are meaningful to us personally, and the memories of our own beloved dead.

The saint under my pillow

When I was a child, I had a small box of 'worry dolls'. These are traditional in Guatemala – they are tiny dolls that children tell their worries to and then tuck under their pillows so that their worries won't scare them at night.

You can make dolls of saints to 'protect' your children. Ask the children to choose 'their' patron saint and then select a way of making dolls (paper dolls, cloth dolls, etc. – a variety of ideas and patterns can be found at <www.allcrafts.net/dolls.htm>). Your children can make their very own patron saint doll, and sleep with it under their pillow, to keep them safe during the night.

Altar of the dead

Many Latin American countries celebrate 'Dia de Los Muertos', the Day of the Dead, on All Souls Day. It is traditional on this day for families to set up altars in their homes to commemorate the dead. You can use a small table, and cover it with a colourful cloth. On it you place the *ofrendas*, the offerings. These traditionally include objects the deceased can use in the afterlife, such as a basin of water (you can connect this to the new life of baptism, if you like) or a razor; photographs of the deceased; and objects they would have liked, such as a favourite food. At dinner, you can remember the people on your altar, and, if you like, share stories about them.

It is also traditional in Mexico to visit the cemetery where loved ones are buried on this day. If you live near the burial place of those you love, this could be a way of celebrating their lives. If not, you might contact local churches with graveyards and see if they need help tending graves that are not cared for by family members.

The Word became flesh

INTRODUCTION

In an ideal world, Christmas Eve would be a time of peaceful, joyful anticipation. Your church staff would have the time and energy to set up and host a three-hour celebration for the church's children, and your families would enthusiastically attend it. It would be a time of relaxation and Christian community, and a meaningful way to mark the transition from Advent to Christmas.

You can stop laughing now.

Given that we live in the real world, where Christmas Eve is full of turkeys that won't defrost properly, relatives with boundary issues, presents that somehow still aren't wrapped or even bought, houses that look as if a tornado has hit them, and over-excited three-year-olds having screaming meltdowns, not to mention vicars in desperate need of a gin and tonic, and dozens of families who have already left your parish to spend Christmas somewhere else, there are several ways of adapting the liturgy and activities for a meaningful Advent/Christmas celebration.

The most straightforward arrangement is:

1 *Fourth Sunday of Advent*: preparation activities and singing practice in Sunday School;

2 *Christmas Eve*: liturgy;

3 *First Sunday after Christmas*: processing activities.

However, you can also transfer the whole thing to the fourth Saturday or Sunday evening of Advent, and include preparation activities, liturgy and processing activities in the standard Family Day format.

This leaves you without a separate children's service on Christmas Eve – whether that's a problem or not will vary from one church to another. This liturgy is fairly long, compared to the others. If you're trying to keep it short, you can cut Part 2.

The liturgy is designed to provide a ritualized transition from Advent to Christmas. It starts with the story of Adam and Eve and the Fall (this can be retold in your own way, or by using the words given in the liturgy, but it should be told by someone who is used to telling stories with the children, e.g. a Sunday School leader), and then moves to the prophecies of salvation and the celebration of Christmas. It is designed to lead directly into a party. The narrative of the Fall can be acted out, using Godly Play figures, Beulah Land feltboard figures, human actors, puppets, etc. But avoid the temptation to make it kitschy – it should be solemn. And focus not on the curse of Adam and Eve, but on the loss of the garden, with its symbolism of innocence and peace.

During the liturgy, the leader will invite the children to draw or write something on their paper hearts (see page 54), which they would like to give to the Baby Jesus. Younger children will probably take this very literally and draw some sort of baby item – a blanket, food, etc. This is fine, as it gets them thinking about Jesus as a real human baby, and encourages care and concern for others. Older children may draw themselves praying, or helping others, or amending a bad habit.

SET-UP AND PREPARATION

It's important to note that this liturgy can include a procession with the entire congregation coming out of their pews and following a child, who is carrying a star ornament, around the sanctuary, finishing in chairs around the chancel. This might take place during the singing of 'O Come, All Ye Faithful'. However, if you have hundreds of people at your service, you may wish to cut the processional aspect of this part. There is also a section at the beginning when children who have had stuffed animals in the pews are invited to come up and place them around the crib. Larger congregations may also wish to limit the number of children who have stuffed animals, so you don't have hundreds of children mobbing your chancel crib scene.

For the liturgy

1 Chairs around the chancel (if you include the procession).

2 A paper heart and some markers or crayons for each child. These can be handed to children as they arrive for the service. You can make your own paper hearts, or use the template from the All Saints/All Souls chapter.

3 The crib scene, with animal figures placed by it, and with human and angel figures nearby but hidden.

4 While the children are writing on the paper hearts, instrumental music should be played. I suggest Beethoven's 'Ode to Joy'. You can use a recording of this piece if you don't have musicians.

5 Whatever props are needed for telling the story of the Fall.

6 The Advent wreath, with central candle.

7 A fire extinguisher, just in case.

8 Stuffed animals in the pews – predators and prey.

9 A star ornament, held on a cuphook screwed into a dowel, and a child to carry it. This child should have practised at least once in advance, as he or she will need to lead the congregation at certain points.

10 Children to read at least one of the lessons – they should practise in advance. It would be better for adults to read the actual Nativity story, so they can pause at the correct times and invite children to come up and place the correct figures in the manger. However, a child can read the 'Comfort, comfort my people' lesson and, if they have been coached in inviting other children to bring up their stuffed animals at the correct time, the lesson of the Peaceable Kingdom. A child can also read the lesson from the Gospel of John ('In the beginning was the word').

11 An organist or pianist, to accompany the singing. Some services (those for Good Friday and Ash Wednesday in particular) can be done a cappella and still be effective. Not this one. The hymns need to be loud and joyful, there needs to be some kind of fanfare or introduction in the lead-in to 'O Come, All Ye Faithful', and you need to have the option of extending organ or piano music to cover the finishing of an action or the movement of the congregation from one place to another, so it's not happening over silence.

For the party afterwards

1 Food. This might include spiced punch, gingerbread, mince pies, etc. (some recipes are given in the 'Extension activities' section).

2 A CD player with a CD of Christmas carols (sacred ones, please – 'Jingle Bell Rock' has no place here), and candles everywhere. The congregation is encouraged to stay and celebrate and share food together, while Christmas carols play in the background. This fellowship is just as much a part of the celebration as the liturgy, so people should be encouraged to stay if they can, and a genuine effort should be made to make it enjoyable.

3 If you have time and energy, games can be played, e.g. pass the parcel, pin the tail on the donkey (the donkey can be carrying Mary to Bethlehem), etc. For a complete list, see 'Extension activities'. If you have a talented pianist, and a piano, you can finish by singing carols.

CHRISTMAS LITURGY

The Word became flesh

PART 1: HUMANITY'S NEED FOR A SAVIOUR

The church is in semi-darkness. The crib scene is set up in front of the altar, but there are no humans or angels in it. We gather in the nave. In the pews are stuffed animals – some predators, some prey. Children are allowed to play with these animals during the first part of the service.

Carol

> O come, O come, Emmanuel
> Redeem thy captive Israel,
> That into exile drear is gone
> Far from the face of God's dear Son.
> > Rejoice! Rejoice! Emmanuel
> > Shall come to thee, O Israel.

Story: The Fall

Reader   In the beginning,
God made the world.
He made a man and a woman,
and put them in a beautiful garden.

They had everything they needed.
They were safe.

But the snake was the most deceitful of all the animals,
and came up to the woman and said,
'Did God say you can't eat of any of the trees in the garden?'

And the woman said,
'We may eat of any of the trees,
but not of the tree in the middle of the garden,
the Tree of the Knowledge of Good and Evil.
For God has said that if we touch this tree,
we will die.'

The snake said,
'You will not die.
If you eat from that tree, you will be *just like God*.
You can do whatever you want.
You'll be just as big and special as God.
You won't have to do what he says any more.
Come on.
Try it.'

So the man and the woman ate
from the Tree of the Knowledge of Good and Evil.

But it didn't make them big and special.

It made them ashamed.

They were ashamed of their thoughts.
They were ashamed of their bodies.
They were ashamed of what they had done.
They wanted God, but were scared of him.

And they couldn't live in the garden any more.
They had to go out into the world,
and work hard,
and feel pain,
and die.

But God did not forget them.
God began the long work of saving them.

And that's our story.

Carol

O come, thou Wisdom from on high
Who madest all in earth and sky,
Creating man from dust and clay:
To us reveal salvation's way.
Rejoice! Rejoice! Emmanuel
Shall come to thee, O Israel.

Reading

Isaiah 11.1–4a, 6–7, 9

Reader   When you hear the words 'The wolf shall dwell with the lamb', you may bring your animals up and place them around the crib.

A reading from the book of the prophet Isaiah.

There shall come forth a shoot from the stump of Jesse, and a branch shall grow out of his roots; and the Spirit of the Lord shall rest upon him, the spirit of wisdom and understanding, the spirit of counsel and might, the spirit of knowledge and the fear of the Lord.

He shall not judge by what his eyes see, or decide by what his ears hear; but with righteousness he shall judge the poor.

The wolf shall dwell with the lamb, and the leopard shall lie down with the kid, and the calf and the lion and the fatling together, and a little child shall lead them. The cow and the bear shall feed; their young shall lie down together, and the lion shall eat straw like the ox.

They shall not hurt or destroy in all my holy mountain; for the earth shall be full of the knowledge of the Lord as the waters cover the seas.

PART 2: WAITING WITH JOYFUL ANTICIPATION

Hymn

What wondrous love is this, O my soul, O my soul?
What wondrous love is this, O my soul?
What wondrous love is this that caused the Lord of bliss
To send this perfect peace to my soul, to my soul,
To send this perfect peace to my soul?

Ye winged seraphs fly, bear the news, bear the news.
Ye winged seraphs fly, bear the news.
Ye winged seraphs fly, like comets through the sky.
Fill vast eternity with the news, with the news,
Fill vast eternity with the news.

Silence is kept.

Reading

Isaiah 40.1–2a, 3–4a, 11

Reader   A reading from the book of the prophet Isaiah.

Comfort, comfort my people, says your God. Speak tenderly to Jerusalem, and cry to her that her warfare is ended, that her iniquity is pardoned.

A voice cries: 'In the wilderness prepare the way of the LORD, make straight in the desert a highway for our God. Every valley shall be lifted up, and every mountain and hill be made low.

And he will feed his flock like a shepherd, he will gather the lambs in his arms, and gently lead those that are with young.'

Carol

On Jordan's bank the Baptist's cry
Announces that the Lord is nigh;
Awake and hearken, for he brings
Glad tidings of the King of kings.

Then cleansed be every breast from sin;
Make straight the way for God within,
Prepare we in our hearts a home
Where such a mighty Guest may come.

Reader   The night is far spent, the day is at hand. Let us therefore cast aside the works of darkness and put on the armour of light.

The leader invites a child to come up and light the central candle on the Advent wreath. The congregation stands.

Reading

John 1.1–5

Reader   A reading from the Gospel according to John.

In the beginning was the Word, and the Word was with God, and the Word was God. He was in the beginning with God; all things were made through him, and without him was not anything made that was made. In him was life, and the life was the light of humankind. The light shines in the darkness, and the darkness has not overcome it.

The child who has lit the Advent wreath lights his or her candle from it, and then lights the leader's candle. The leader and the child then go to the front row of the congregation and light two candles there. Please light the candle of the person seated next to you or behind you when the light reaches you. As the candles are lit, we sing 'Silent Night'.

Carol

Silent night, holy night,
All is calm, all is bright
Round yon virgin mother and child.
Holy infant so tender and mild,
Sleep in heavenly peace,
Sleep in heavenly peace.

Silent night, holy night!
Shepherds quake at the sight;
Glories stream from heaven afar,
Heavenly hosts sing Alleluia!
Christ, the Saviour is born,
Christ, the Saviour is born.

Silent night, holy night,
Son of God, love's pure light;

Radiant beams from thy holy face
With the dawn of redeeming grace.
Jesus, Lord, at Thy birth,
Jesus, Lord, at Thy birth.

PART 3: TELLING THE STORY

Reading

Luke 2.1, 3–7

Reader   A reading from the Gospel according to Luke.

In those days a decree went out from Caesar Augustus that all the world should be enrolled. And all went to be enrolled, each to his own city. And Joseph also went up from Galilee, from the city of Nazareth, to Judea, to the city of David, which is called Bethlehem, because he was of the house and lineage of David, to be enrolled with Mary, his betrothed, who was with child.

(A child is invited to place the figures of Mary and Joseph in the crib scene.)

And while they were there, the time came for her to be delivered. And she gave birth to her first-born son and wrapped him in swaddling clothes, and laid him in a manger, because there was no place for them in the inn.

(A child is invited to lay the figure of the Christ Child in the manger.)

Carol

O little town of Bethlehem,
How still we see thee lie!
Above thy deep and dreamless sleep
The silent stars go by;
Yet in thy dark streets shineth
The everlasting Light;
The hopes and fears of all the years
Are met in thee tonight.

O morning stars, together
Proclaim the holy birth
And praises sing to God, the King,
And Peace to men on earth.
For Christ is born of Mary
And gathered all above,
While mortals sleep, the angels keep
Their watch of wondering love.

Reading

Luke 2.8–16

Reader   A reading from the Gospel according to Luke.

And in that region there were shepherds out in the field, keeping watch over their flock by night.

(A child is invited to place the figures of the shepherds in the crib scene.)

And an angel of the Lord appeared to them, and the glory of the Lord shone around them, and they were filled with fear. And the angel said to them, 'Be not afraid; for behold, I bring you good news of a great joy which will come to all the people; for to you is born this day in the city of David a Saviour, who is Christ the Lord. And this will be a sign for you: you will find a babe wrapped in swaddling clothes and lying in a manger.' And suddenly there was with the angel a multitude of the heavenly host praising God and saying, 'Glory to God in the highest, and on earth peace among those with whom he is pleased!'

(A child is invited to place the figure(s) of the angel(s) in the crib scene.)

When the angels went away from them into heaven, the shepherds said to one another, 'Let us go over to Bethlehem and see this thing that has happened, which the Lord has made known to us.' And they went with haste, and found Mary and Joseph, and the babe lying in a manger.

PART 4: CELEBRATING

The lights in the church are switched on, and the candles extinguished. A child carrying the star ornament, followed by the leaders of the service, comes down from the chancel and down the centre aisle. The congregation processes around the church, ending up in the chairs around the chancel, close to the crib scene.

Carol

O come, all ye faithful, joyful and triumphant,
O come ye, O come ye, to Bethlehem.
Come and behold Him, born the King of angels:

> *Refrain:*
> *O come, let us adore Him,*
> *O come, let us adore Him,*
> *O come, let us adore Him,*
> *Christ the Lord.*

Sing, choirs of angels, sing in exultation;
Sing, all ye citizens of heaven above!
Glory to God in the highest:

> *Refrain*

See how the shepherds, summoned to His cradle,
Leaving their flocks, draw nigh to gaze;
We too will thither bend our joyful footsteps:

Refrain

Leader   At Christmas, angels opened the gates from heaven to earth, and brought the peace of
God to all people. The peace of the Lord be always with you!

All   **And also with you.**

Leader   Let us offer one another a sign of Christ's peace.

At the conclusion of the peace:

Carol

In the bleak midwinter, frosty wind made moan,
Earth stood hard as iron, water like a stone;
Snow had fallen, snow on snow, snow on snow,
In the bleak midwinter, long ago.

Our God, Heaven cannot hold Him, nor earth sustain;
Heaven and earth shall flee away when He comes to reign.
In the bleak midwinter a stable place sufficed
The Lord God Almighty, Jesus Christ.

Angels and archangels may have gathered there,
Cherubim and seraphim thronged the air;
But His mother only, in her maiden bliss,
Worshipped the beloved with a kiss.

What can I give Him, poor as I am?
If I were a shepherd, I would bring a lamb;
If I were a Wise Man, I would do my part;
Yet what I can I give Him: give my heart.

*The leader invites the children to draw or write something on their paper hearts, which they would like
to give to the Baby Jesus. As instrumental music plays, the children make their drawings and bring them
forward to lay around the crib scene.*

During the following reading, the child carrying the star comes to the front of the chancel.

Reading

Isaiah 9.2, 6

Leader   A reading from the book of the prophet Isaiah.

The people who walked in darkness have seen a great light. Those who dwelt in the land
of deep darkness, on them has light shined. For unto us a child is born, unto us a son is
given, and the government shall be upon his shoulders, and his name shall be called
Wonderful Counsellor, Mighty God, the Everlasting Father, the Prince of Peace.

Carol

Hark! The herald angels sing,
'Glory to the newborn King!
Peace on earth, and mercy mild,
God and sinners reconciled.'
Joyful, all ye nations, rise,
Join the triumph of the skies;
With the angelic host proclaim:
'Christ is born in Bethlehem.'
Hark! The herald angels sing,
'Glory to the newborn King!'

Christ, by highest heav'n adored;
Christ the everlasting Lord!
Late in time behold Him come,
Offspring of a Virgin's womb.
Veiled in flesh the Godhead see;
Hail the incarnate Deity,
Pleased as man with man to dwell,
Jesus, our Emmanuel.
Hark! The herald angels sing,
'Glory to the newborn King!'

Hail the heav'n-born Prince of Peace!
Hail the Son of Righteousness!
Light and life to all He brings,
Ris'n with healing in His wings.
Mild He lays His glory by,
Born that man no more may die,
Born to raise the sons of earth,
Born to give them second birth.
Hark! The herald angels sing,
'Glory to the newborn King!'

During the final verse, the child carrying the star starts down the centre aisle. The congregation follows. The star leads us to where a Christmas feast is laid out.

Leader   Alleluia! Alleluia! In the tender compassion of our God, the dawn from on high has broken upon us! Let us celebrate the joy of Christmas together.

We stay and celebrate together.

ADDING A EUCHARIST

The best place to put a Eucharist in this liturgy would be immediately after the congregation have drawn their offerings on the paper hearts. The bringing forward of the paper hearts, therefore, could take the liturgical place of the offertory, and lead directly into the Eucharist.

ADAPTATIONS FOR SCHOOLS

- **Bringing forward the animals for the Peaceable Kingdom.** You can choose several children at the beginning of the liturgy to do this, instead of having all the children participate.

- **Bringing forward the paper hearts to the manger.** Since this is a reflective activity, all children should participate in it. Children should bring their own pens from their classrooms. Teachers or children could stand at the door with paper hearts, as the children come in, and hand the hearts out to each child. Place baskets by the doors, and as the children go out, they can drop their paper hearts into the basket. You could then use these to make a display by your crib scene.

- **Processing around the church during 'O Come, All Ye Faithful'.** This could easily be cut, and the hymn sung from where you stand.

- **Candles.** A dozen or so responsible children from Years 5 and 6 could sit at the front, on benches facing inward, holding candles. This would be enough to create a feeling of candlelit calm, while not risking fire.

- **Going out together to the party.** Children could go straight from the liturgy to separate parties in their classrooms.

EXTENSION ACTIVITIES

Preparation activities

Christmas is hard. Children are over-committed and excitable, and by the time they reach the age of eight or nine, they know the story of Christmas so well it's sometimes hard to enthuse them about it, or enable them to see it as the amazing good news that it is. And honestly, who can blame them? After all, why should we care that some woman had a baby two thousand years ago? Isn't it more exciting to dream about what presents will be under the tree, or to plan your outfit for the big Christmas party, or to stuff yourself with mince pies until you can't move?

The goal of these activities is therefore to put Christmas into context, so that children will understand the significance of the Incarnation.

Gertrud Mueller Nelson's book *To Dance With God* includes some excellent suggestions for celebrating Advent with children, building up anticipation of the religious elements of Christmas as well as the secular ones.[1] And many churches go carol-singing around their parish at Christmas time. Here are a few more, which can be used as a way of preparing children for the Christmas liturgy.

Kinaesthetic

A walk through the stories used traditionally in lessons and carols. This activity is best done by the group as a whole, not as one choice among many, as it requires movement from one space to another, and builds the narrative as it goes.

You can begin by acting out the story of Adam and Eve. I've successfully made a tree out of spray-painted twigs stuck into a flowerpot full of sand, and hung apple Christmas tree ornaments on it. You can wrap a stuffed snake around the tree.

Briefly narrate the next part of the story – the people lost the beautiful garden and had to live in the desert. It was hard work, and there was lots of pain and suffering. God called one man, Abraham, and his wife Sarah, and promised them that they would be the father and mother of his chosen people. He gave them a son, Isaac, even though they were old and had given up hope.

You can then tell the story of the sacrifice of Isaac, using a sand tray and a few Godly Play figures (or Playmobil, or doll's house dolls in robes) and an altar made out of blocks. Now would be a good time for reflective wondering questions on the stories so far, both of which are difficult and full of questions about why the world is the way it is, why there is sin and death, etc.

Now briefly narrate the rest of the story as far as the prophecies – Isaac had children, and grandchildren, and they became the people of Israel. They were slaves in Egypt, but God set them free. He brought them into the Promised Land, and gave them the ten commandments to show them how to live. He sent them prophets and kings and teachers, but the people still fought among themselves, lied, cheated, killed one another, and disobeyed God's rules.

Next you can build the Peaceable Kingdom. Make available a variety of stuffed animals, and ask the children to separate them into predators and prey. Each child should then choose one animal and go back to the tree. Remove the fruit ornaments, and hang a rose ornament in the tree (Jesus is sometimes called the 'rose of Jesse's stem', the new life coming from the lineage of the Kings of Israel). Explain this to the children, then read the prophecy and tell the children to bring up their animals and place them around the tree when they hear the words 'The wolf shall dwell with the lamb'. (This will be repeated at the actual liturgy, except the tree will be replaced by the

Figure 5 *A Nativity scene surrounded by animals of the Peaceable Kingdom*

manger scene – the metaphorical foretelling of Jesus replaced by the actual Jesus.) You can then have some more wondering questions, about peace, living together, an end to violence, etc.

Next tell the story of the Annunciation. Choose a child to be Mary, and play the role of the Angel yourself. I've had great success acting out this story this way, by palming a party popper so the children don't see it, and letting it off at the moment the Angel appears to Mary. The shock and surprise on the children's faces is genuine – similar to what Mary's reaction to the angel must have been like!

Explain that when God chose Mary to be the mother of Jesus, he was doing something new. God himself was coming to share our life, to be a child like us, to live and die as one of us, to defeat death and share new life with all of us.

Do *not* continue to the story of the Nativity. Leave the children in suspense!

Creative

Give each child a square of fabric and fabric pens (or felt, scissors and glue). Tell them you're going to make a timeline, showing the story of God's people from the beginning of the Bible to the birth of Jesus. Say, 'In the beginning, God made the world – what happened next?' Keep notes on a large piece of paper or interactive whiteboard, so the children are clear on the chronology. Focus on:

• Eden

• desert patriarchs

• Egypt

• the desert

- the Promised Land

- the Babylonian exile

- the prophecies of a saviour.

Allow the children to choose which story they want to depict. They design their square, and the leader, or a parent volunteer, will take home the squares and sew them together. The resulting frieze can then be hung on the altar during the Christmas Eve liturgy.

Verbal

Print out pictures of Old Testament scenes that show God's attempts to draw humankind to himself, and human sinfulness. Avoid clipart – stick to paintings, icons, etc., that have some depth of imagery to them. A good selection would be Adam and Eve, Cain and Abel, the rainbow and Noah's Ark, the Exodus, and an image of the Peaceable Kingdom or the rose of Jesse's tree, to tie in with the prophecies.

Hang them on the wall in chronological order. Divide sheets of A3 paper into three columns and place one under each picture. Title the columns 'What I can see', 'What I think is happening' and 'Questions I have about this picture'. Let children look at the pictures in detail and write their ideas and questions on the A3 paper. Come together at the end to share what they wrote and address some of the questions.

Ask 'Why are we looking at these stories at Christmas?' and discuss.

Service-oriented

This activity is best for older children, who may already have a grasp of the story's context and the significance of the Incarnation. It also requires some preparation, in that you need to research an appropriate charity to be the recipient of what you make.

Paint a wooden vegetable box brown, and fill it with straw (I stole some from our Harvest decorations and kept it until Christmas). Place a baby doll in the manger, wrapped up in fabric. Copy out the following Bible verses and place them in envelopes:

1 'The Spirit of the Lord is upon me, for he has anointed me to bring Good News to the poor. He has sent me to proclaim that captives will be released, that the blind will see, that the oppressed will be set free' (Luke 4.18).

2 'What does the LORD require of you but to do justice, and to love kindness, and to walk humbly with your God?' (Micah 6.8).

3 'When the Son of man comes in his glory, and all the angels with him, then he will sit on his glorious throne. Before him will be gathered all the nations, and he will separate them one from another as a shepherd separates the sheep from the goats, and he will place the sheep at his right hand, but the goats at the left. Then the King will say to those at his right hand, "Come, O blessed of my Father, inherit the kingdom prepared for you; for I was hungry and you gave me food, I was thirsty and you gave me drink, I was a stranger and you welcomed me, I was naked and you clothed me, I was sick and you visited me, I was in prison and you came to me." Then the righteous will answer him, "Lord, when did we see you hungry and feed thee, or thirsty and give thee drink? And when did we see thee a stranger and welcome thee, or naked and clothe thee? And when did we see thee sick or in prison and visit thee?" And the King will answer them, "Truly, I say to you, as you did it to one of the least of these my brethren, you did it to me"' (Matthew 25.31–40).

Tie the envelopes with gift ribbon or place bows on them, so they are 'presents'. Place the presents in the manger.

Explain to the children that the baby Jesus was God's gift to humanity, to share our life. Ask three children who are confident readers to come up and open the gifts in the manger and read them out.

Ask the children – who do you think Jesus means by 'the least of these'? Who are the people our society overlooks? Homeless people? Children? The poor? The elderly? The mentally ill? Prisoners? Take suggestions from the children. Point out that Jesus himself was a poor child without a safe home.

For your activity, make Christmas cards to give to a local charity that is providing a Christmas dinner/party for its clients. If your church does one, that's even better. Your local branches of Shelter, Refuge, Action for Children or Age UK are good places to start. Your local council may also be able to give you ideas.

If you are able to, encourage the children to bring a present to this activity as well. Then their card can go with their present.

Multi-sensory

- Make a sheet with symbols of Christmas and print out two copies. Some symbols you could use are:

a star	Joseph
an angel	a shepherd
a manger	a stable
a rose	Herod
Mary	a candle.

Use thick card, or glue card to the back of each sheet so you can't see through the paper. Turn them upside down, and children can play Memory with them, turning over two cards at once and setting them aside if they match. If they don't match, they turn the cards face down again and try again.

- Take a selection of religiously themed Christmas tree decorations (star, angel, baby in manger, etc.) and place each one in a shoebox. Cut a hand-sized hole in one end of the shoebox and invite children to push their hands through the hole and feel each ornament to work out what it is.

- Similarly, you can have a 'guess that smell' table. Myrrh and frankincense are easily available from Amazon, and you can add Christmas spices such as ginger and nutmeg. If you have some good aromatic old straw, that works too! Place each one in a clean, washed plastic food container (ricotta cheese tubs are perfect) and punch holes in the top. Make a label saying what each one is and stick it to the bottom of each tub. Children can smell each one and guess what it is, then check the bottom to see if they're right.

Las Posadas

You can also hold a *Las Posadas* procession as your preparation for the liturgy.

Las Posadas (Spanish for 'the lodgings') is a Mexican Christmas tradition, during which children re-enact the journey of Mary and Joseph from Nazareth to Bethlehem. It takes place over several nights, traditionally from 16 to 24 December, and a different house hosts it each night. The children knock on door after door, singing a traditional song about pilgrims and asking for lodging. At each house they are refused, until they find the 'right' door. The 'innkeeper' at this house invites them in, and holds a party. Statues of Mary and Joseph are carried, and all the other participants carry lighted candles as they go from house to house. Each house on the Posadas journey is decorated, and its path is lined with lanterns in paper bags.

For a wonderful introduction to this custom, read children Tomie de Paola's book, *The Night of Las Posadas*.[2] Set in modern-day Santa Fe, this book tells the story of Lupe and Roberto, who are chosen to play Jose and Maria in their church's *Las Posadas* celebration. But their lorry breaks down and two mysterious strangers appear to play the parts instead. Both an introduction to the tradition and a story about the wonder of Christmas, this book is great.

Re-creating *Las Posadas* is a time-consuming project which requires sustained help from a large number of volunteers and sustained commitment from the children. If you want to adapt this tradition for your church, I suggest you do it in one of the following ways:

- Hold a *Posada* on one night only. You could even do it as the lead-up to the liturgy, with children knocking on the doors of several parishioners, who refuse them entrance but then join the procession, and finishing by knocking on the door of the church, where the vicar then invites them in, to begin the liturgy.

- If your church has a school connected to it, hold a school Posadas celebration. Choose several children to be Mary and Joseph, and choose a different class to hold the *Las Posadas* party each day. Send Mary and Joseph around the school (accompanied by a teaching assistant), knocking on each classroom door and being told to go away, until they find the class that hosts that day's party. Children can make Posada decorations as part of their Art or RE lessons leading up to *Las Posadas*, and they can make food as part of their DT or Science lessons.

Paper lanterns

Paper lanterns are simple for children to make and remarkably effective, while allowing lots of room for creativity. They can be made as part of a *Las Posadas* celebration (they are used to light the paths leading up to the houses in the procession) or as a Sunday School craft to prepare for/process the liturgy in this chapter.

If the lanterns are not being used for *Las Posadas*, children can take them home and place them in the windows of their house, to light the darkness of winter. The lanterns are perfectly safe as long as children are attended while they are alight. One parent told me that in the thirty seconds her back was turned, her child managed to set his lantern on fire and take part of the tablecloth with it. In making hundreds of paper lanterns, this is the only accident I've heard of. But make sure parents know that as long as the candle is lighted, they should not turn their back on their child!

You will need:

- white paper party bags (available from party supply stores or online)

- sand

- tealights

- paint.

Give each child a paper bag, which they are encouraged to paint with symbols from the Christmas story (this can be done either in advance, after a reading of the Christmas story, if the lanterns

Figure 6 *A display of paper lanterns*

will be used in the liturgy or as a processing activity afterwards). Make sure the children decorate more than one side! When the bags are dry, drop a few handfuls of sand in the bottom – this will hold the bag in place and keep the tealight from slipping around. Light a tealight and set it in the bottom of the bag. The candle will shine through the paint, illuminating the children's decorations.

Processing activities

The liturgy is designed to move from solemn contemplation to joyful celebration – therefore the most appropriate way to follow it up would be with a party of some sort. This allows children to absorb the idea that the type of joy we normally associate with secular Christmas celebrations has its place in the sacred as well, that it's not just the presents and the dinner and the general hype of Christmas that makes us want to shout and sing and play and run around, but also the fact of God made incarnate, the fulfilment of God's promise of a Saviour. Children should come out of the liturgy on a high note, with the release of tension that occurs when the lights are switched on and we switch from singing Advent hymns to Christmas ones. Take that energy and joy, and celebrate it!

If you want to give children opportunities for creative activities during the party, you can find some suggestions later on in this section. But first, here are some ideas for a party that retains the integrity of a sacred Christmas celebration.

Games for the celebration after the liturgy

Pass the parcel

Make every present in your parcels a Christmas tree ornament with sacred significance. Meaningful Chocolate (<www.meaningfulchristmas.co.uk>) sells sets of six chocolate ornaments with scenes from the Christmas story on them. You could also use a lamb, a star, a crown or a fish. Have some extra ornaments on hand in case there are children who don't get one.

Pin the tail on the donkey

Print out a picture of Mary and Joseph travelling to Bethlehem, and make some donkey tails out of grey and black paper. Put Blu-Tack on the back of them and play this Christmas-themed version.

Charades

Instead of having people make up their own, prepare a basket full of Christmas-themed charades challenges, such as 'the three kings', 'the manger', 'the angel appearing to the shepherds', 'sheep', 'the star of Bethlehem' and so on. Children choose one sight unseen and then have to act it out until someone guesses what it is.

Piñata

This is a traditional part of Mexican Christmas celebrations. The piñata is a cardboard sculpture filled with sweets. Children take turns hitting it with a stick until it breaks and scatters sweets everywhere. Children then rush to pick up as many sweets as they can. (You can get piñatas from most party supply shops.) This can be difficult with groups of children who are inclined to fight with each other – a wonderful volunteer at my Sunday School came up with an idea for Easter Egg hunts that is easily transferrable here. Every child has a cup, and can only take as many sweets as his or her cup can hold. After that, if the child wants to keep picking up sweets, he can, but must give them to a child whose cup is not yet full.

Scavenger hunt

This is a good way of familiarizing children with the church building, and has the added benefit of being lots of fun with minimal preparation.

Create a list of items related to Christmas that can be broadly interpreted – for example, a 'star' can mean a Christmas tree ornament shaped like a star, a kneeler with a star on it, a photo taken of a stained-glass window with a star in it, a Christmas book with a star in it, etc. Children form teams and are given a set amount of time to find as many items on the list as possible. The team finding the most items wins. Adults can be stationed in different parts of the church to supervise behaviour in that area, or each team can have an adult chaperone. Make sure that you state *clearly*, and at the *beginning* of the scavenger hunt, any rules about where the children aren't allowed to go, what they are or aren't allowed to touch, etc. It helps to give each team a camera, so if there's an item they want to include which they can't pick up and carry back (e.g. a stained-glass window, a carved pew end, as opposed to, say, an icon or a kneeler or a candle), they can take a picture of it. You will also need to clarify whether one item is allowed to be counted for more than one category.

As for the question of how to reward the winning team without upsetting those who haven't won – my standard technique is that you get one prize for participating, and a second prize for winning. That way, everyone gets *something*, but the winners are still rewarded.

Here's a suggested list for a Christmas scavenger hunt. You may need to amend it for your own building:

a star	a gift
a tree	a sheep
a rose	something you would take on a journey
a picture of a mother and child	something a baby needs
a light source	something you need in winter
an angel	a jewel
a donkey	something to help you celebrate.
a crown	

Recipes for a Christmas Eve feast

Making these can be part of the children's preparation for the liturgy. You can either choose a recipe or two to make in Sunday School on the fourth Sunday of Advent, or you can send a recipe card home with each child and ask them to make it at home and bring it in. This helps give children ownership of the celebration, and instils in them the idea that church is something to be involved in beyond just turning up on Sunday morning.

For the spiced punch recipe, see the Harvest Festival chapter.

GINGERBREAD

Makes around 40 medium-sized biscuits

These biscuits are delicious – crispy on the outside, chewy in the middle, and with a rich wintry ginger taste. The recipe is easy for children to make (ask them to wash their hands first).

To lend a religious touch, you can use cookie cutters in shapes appropriate to the season – stars, hearts, angels, even a church! For a good selection of religious cookie cutters, go to <www.cakescookiesandcraftsshop.co.uk>. Stars, Mary, Joseph, angels, churches and more can be found in their Christmas section, while they also have a cup and cross in their Religious section.

For the gingerbread:

350 g plain flour

1 teaspoon bicarbonate of soda

3 teaspoons ground ginger

100 g soft butter or margarine

175 g soft light brown sugar

4 tablespoons golden syrup

2 teaspoons milk

1 egg

For the icing:

150 g soft butter

300 g icing sugar

2 tablespoons milk

food colouring (optional)

1 Grease 1 large baking tray or 2 small ones, then preheat oven to 190° C/gas mark 5.

2 In an electric mixer or a large bowl, place the flour, bicarbonate of soda and ginger, then add the butter. Mix the ingredients.

3 Add the brown sugar and then stir in the syrup, milk and egg so it makes a firm dough. (You may need to stick your hands in the bowl and swoosh the mixture together, using the heat of your hands to help soften the butter so the dough forms well. Children will love helping with this part.)

4 Roll out the dough mixture to about 5 mm thick and cut out your shapes.

5 Place the biscuits on the greased tray, leaving a little space between each one as they will spread.

6 Cook for 8–10 minutes until golden brown.

7 Meanwhile, make icing. Mix 1 part softened butter to 2 parts icing sugar. Add 1–2 tablespoons of milk per 150 g of butter, and any food colouring you want.

8 Leave the biscuits to cool on a wire rack. Once cooled decorate with icing.

MINCE PIES

Makes 12

The pastry, on its own, also makes delicious biscuits, particularly when sprinkled with sugar and cinnamon.

500 g mincemeat	*75 g ground almonds*
200 g plain flour, sifted	*1 large egg, beaten*
40 g golden caster sugar	*splash of milk to glaze*
125 g unsalted butter, diced	*icing sugar and cinnamon (optional)*

1 Preheat the oven to 200° C/gas mark 6.

2 Lightly grease a 12-hole baking tin.

3 Place the mincemeat in a bowl and give it a quick stir so that any liquid is distributed evenly.

4 In a food processor place the flour, sugar, butter and almonds and process until the mix looks like fine breadcrumbs, then slowly add the egg and mix again.

5 Gather the mixture together in your hands and roll into a ball, then thinly roll out the pastry onto a floured surface. Cut out 12 circles with a pastry cutter (you can also use an upside-down drinking glass to do this!). Press 1 circle of pastry into each of the 12 holes in the baking tin. Press gently down, then fill each with mincemeat.

6 Next cut another 12 circles out of the remaining pastry, this time making them a tiny bit smaller. Place these smaller circles over the mincemeat and firm around the edges so they stick together.

7 Make a small slit on top of each of the 12 mince pies and brush each one with a little milk to glaze.

8 Bake the pies in the oven for around 20 minutes until golden brown. Remove them from the oven and let them cool. You can even sprinkle a little icing sugar and cinnamon over each one to decorate before serving.

Creative processing activities

You can do these during the party that follows the liturgy, or in your first Sunday School session after the liturgy.

Candle decorating

One way to work with symbols and imagery is to buy candles which the children can decorate with symbols of Christmas or pictures from the Christmas story. Baker Ross sells pens that contain liquid wax, which can be used to decorate candles. This activity requires thick pillar candles, which can stand up on their own, so children can draw all around them and then leave them to dry standing up. Under no circumstances should children try to decorate tall, thin candles using these pens. The wax takes a long time to dry and therefore, if the candle is not fat enough to stand up, you will a) only be able to decorate one side of it, as it will need to dry lying down, and b) most likely end up smearing wax all over the table, even if you're careful.

Myriad Natural Toys stocks thin sheets of coloured beeswax that children can cut into shapes and stick straight on to candles. If you use this method, ensure the candles have as high a beeswax content as possible – this makes them stickier, and the decorative wax will adhere to them better.

If you'd like the children to *make* the candles, kits are available from many educational suppliers; however, this doesn't give them a chance to work with the symbols and images of the liturgy and the Christmas story.

Illustrating the readings

Print out the text of the readings from the liturgy. Use large type but make sure you leave plenty of white space. Provide a variety of drawing materials (felt tips, oil pastels, charcoal, chalk, crayons, paint) for children to use to illustrate them. The illustrations can be made into a display, or used to make the service sheet for next year's liturgy. This activity helps reinforce the texts and imagery in the children's minds, as they tend to read more closely when they have a purpose for reading – in this case, finding images to use for their pictures. The fact that they have already heard these texts in a liturgical context helps make the task less daunting for them, and links the text, in their minds, with all the emotions and sensory experiences of the worship service.

Making a manger scene

There are a variety of ways for children to make their own manger scene, which can be taken home and used year after year.

- Crafts of Russia (<http://craftsofrussia.co.uk/paint%20your%20own.htm>) makes blank seven-piece nesting doll sets, which can be painted to resemble the characters from a Nativity scene (three kings, Mary, Joseph and a shepherd or angel, with the baby Jesus as the smallest doll).

- Many shops on craft superstore Etsy (<www.etsy.com>) sell blank wooden dolls, which children can turn into Nativity scene characters. Etsy is an international shop, but most sellers of these dolls (search for 'unfinished wooden dolls' on the site) are in the USA – but shipping to the UK is relatively inexpensive, and the Etsy website automatically shows all prices in sterling when you use a UK-based computer.

- You can make figures out of craft sticks, pipe cleaners and felt, sticking each in a base of modelling clay to make them stand up.

- The cheapest – though not the longest-lasting – way to make a homemade Nativity scene is to use a toilet-roll centre for the body of each figure, and provide paper which children can cut into circles and glue onto the roll centre to make a head. You could also use polystyrene balls for the heads. Felt in different colours can be used for the bodies.

- A shoebox can be made into a stable.

Banner-making

Banner-making instructions are in the All Saints/All Souls chapter. Some ideas for Christmas banners include:

- the Annunciation

- the Nativity

- the Three Kings

- the Peaceable Kingdom

- part of the service, e.g. pictures of the children holding candles, accompanied by the words 'Silent Night, Holy Night'.

EXTENSIONS FOR HOME

Both the recipes on pages 73–4 can become part of your family Christmas traditions. But there are many other ways of celebrating a sacred Christmas in the home. One thing you may like to do is create your own Advent calendar.

Advent calendars have become so mainstream that they have lost their religious focus. I have spent more time than I'd care to wading through displays full of Disney character Advent calendars to find a religiously themed one that wasn't hideously tacky. Also, while it's nice to have a ready-made chocolate waiting for you every day, I'm not sure exactly what spiritual benefit the sweets have. How are they helping children prepare their hearts and minds for Christmas?

When I was a child, charities would send us Advent and Lenten calendars as a way of fundraising – each day was marked by an activity that led to a certain amount of money being set aside for the charity. A few charities still do these, including Christian Aid, but if you'd like to involve the children in choosing which charity they raise money for (or choose a local one that doesn't make a calendar), I've written a generic one that you can use at home or in church.

I'm not suggesting you dispense with a traditional Advent calendar altogether (though I would recommend you get the delicious Fairtrade one from Traidcraft, which helps poor farmers as well as being beautiful and having high-quality chocolate), but you might consider using the following more thought-provoking calendar (see pages 78–9) as well. If you're feeling crafty and would like to turn it into an actual calendar with doors, feel free – there are some ideas in the Ash Wednesday chapter for making Lenten calendars, and there are many tutorials online for how to make your own Advent calendar. But this is designed more to be a daily devotional activity – the family can read the day's task together and then do whatever counting and gathering of money is needed.

On the first Sunday of Advent, choose a charity that you and your children wish to support. Set up a box for your contributions (you can decorate it with symbols of Advent if you'd like). You might consider a charity that has particular application to Christmas, such as a children's charity or a homeless charity.

Like the Lenten calendar, each week focuses on a different theme. The first day of each week follows the themes of Hope, Peace, Joy and Love; the following days follow the themes of the Old Testament, the Prophets, John the Baptist, and Mary. Since the date of the first Sunday of Advent changes from year to year, I have made the calendar to cover the 24 days of December, instead of the whole season of Advent – each 'week', therefore, is six days, which may or may not begin on a Monday.

As with the Lenten calendar, on days that call for you to count the number of children in your family, you may include children who have died, or, if you are grieving miscarriages, you may count those children as well.

On Boxing Day, open your collection box and count up how much you've contributed throughout Advent, then donate it to your chosen charity.

An Advent calendar

December

		3	4	5	6
Week 1	**1: Hope** Make a list of the things you hope to receive this Christmas. Put 2p in your box for each item on your list. Pray for people who are poor, and may not have many Christmas presents this year.	**2: Old Testament** Abraham and Sarah hoped for a child, and believed God's promise that they would have one, and would be the father and mother of God's chosen people. Put 10p in the box for every child in your family.	God's people were slaves in Egypt. They weren't able to choose what work to do. Your education gives you the freedom to choose your path. Give 5p for every teacher you have, in school or in other lessons.	God's people were set free from slavery in Egypt and lived in the desert for 40 years. When they needed food, God provided manna, the food of angels. Give 10p for every meal you have today.	After 40 years in the desert, the people came into the Promised Land, a land flowing with milk and honey. Give 10p for every container of milk or honey in your house.	God sent the people prophets, to tell them God's plan for them. The prophets told of a Messiah, who would set God's people free from sin. Read Isaiah 9.2–6 and give 5p for every name given to the Messiah.
		9	10	11	12
Week 2	**7: Peace** Make a list of things that make you angry. Then, next to each one, think of something you can do to help you stay peaceful when that happens. Give 2p for every peaceful action/ thought on your list. Pray for people who live in countries where there is fighting.	**8: Prophets** The prophet Isaiah compared the Messiah to a rose growing out of a dead tree. Give 10p for every plant in your house.	Isaiah also said the Messiah would take on our sins. He compared sins to diseases. Give 5p for every box or bottle of medicine in your house.	The prophets said that when the Messiah comes, it will be like a light shining in darkness. Give 5p for every light bulb in your house.	The prophet Micah said that the Lord requires us to do justice and love mercy. Think of anything kind anyone has done for you today. Give 5p for each occasion you can think of.	In ancient times, kings were anointed, or sprinkled, with oil. The word 'Messiah' means 'anointed one' and many of the prophets talk about the Messiah as 'the Lord's anointed one'. Give 5p for every container of oil in your house.

Week 3	**13: Joy** Make a list of everything that makes you happy. Give 2p for every item on it. Pray in thanksgiving to God for everything on your list.	**14: John the Baptist** John the Baptist was Jesus' cousin. Give 2p for every cousin you have. If you have no cousins, give 10p.	**15** When John the Baptist was born, his father sang a song of praise to God. Think of your favourite hymns and give 5p for every one you can think of.	**16** John the Baptist lived in the desert, eating locusts and wild honey. People thought he was strange, but they came to listen to him talk because the word of God was in him. Today, remember to pay attention to people who seem different from you. God might be in their words too.	**17** John the Baptist said, 'I baptize you with water for repentance. But after me will come one who is more powerful than I, whose sandals I am not fit to carry. He will baptize you with the Holy Spirit and with fire.' Give 2p for every tap in your house and 5p for every fireplace.	**18** John the Baptist told the people to get ready because the Messiah was coming. Think of all the things you do to get ready for Christmas, and give 5p for each one. Then think about what you can do to make your heart and mind ready for Jesus to be born.
Week 4	**19: Love** Make a list of everybody you love. Give 2p for every person/animal on the list. Give thanks to God for everyone on your list, and pray for them.	**20: Mary** An angel appeared to Mary and told her she would be the mother of God's son. Give 2p for every picture or statue of an angel in your house. Include any angels on Christmas cards you have received.	**21** Jesus was born to a poor family. Today, 4 million children in the UK still live in poverty.[1] Many live in cramped housing, without enough room. Give 5p for every room in your house. If your parents or carers are worried about money, talk to your vicar, teacher, or another adult you trust.	**22** Mary was very young when Jesus was born, and it was probably hard for her. Find out how old your mum was when she gave birth to you or adopted you, and give 1p for every year of her age then. If you live with someone other than your mum, find out how old they were when you came to live with them and do the same.	**23** Mary and Joseph had to go to Egypt after Jesus was born, to escape from King Herod. There are almost 100,000 children in schools in the UK who have had to leave their own countries to be safe.[2] Think of all the people who take care of you and protect you, and give 5p for every person you can think of.	**24** Jesus was born in a stable, without doctors or midwives. Give 10p for every doctor, nurse or midwife you know.

[1] Source: End Child Poverty.

[2] Source: Research Consortium on the Education of Asylum-Seeker and Refugee Children, Cambridge University.

There Is a Season (London: SPCK). Copyright © Margaret Pritchard Houston 2013.

EPIPHANY

And we have seen his glory

INTRODUCTION

Epiphany is a festival that often gets lost, coming so close after Christmas and often being seen as little more than the postscript to the Christmas story itself – 'and then, twelve days later, three Kings arrived and gave Jesus presents'. Not very exciting, compared to Christmas morning, is it?

But Epiphany is celebrated as a major feast in many parts of the world, and celebrating Epiphany is a good way to look at the Christmas story afresh – an epiphany is a revelation, a discovery. How is the Christ Child a revelation to us? What are we discovering when we come to the manger? The Christmas liturgy in this book focuses on the lead-up to the Christmas story – the fallen nature of humanity, the promises of the prophets, Mary and Joseph's journey to Bethlehem. This Epiphany pageant focuses on what the Incarnation means in our own lives, makes a bridge from the birth of Christ to his death, and tells of the promise of salvation that Jesus gives to us. It relates the humanity of Jesus to the struggles of our own lives.

SET-UP AND PREPARATION

This liturgy is actually closer to a pageant than to an ordinary service, and will require some preparation but not much. You will need a rehearsal (you can even have it on the day of the liturgy), and I suggest having a small and unobtrusive music stand onstage with a script on it, so Mary won't have to memorize her lines. The Kings can have scrolls from which they read their lines.

Because of this, the liturgy is laid out not as an order of service, but as a playscript, with spaces in which I have given several choices for hymns. You should not distribute this as a service sheet.

You will need:

Actors

Young Mary (can be a teenager)

Elder Mary

Joseph (just stands there)

three Kings (need to be competent singers)

reader(s) – there is only one reading, but it can be split between several people

a solo singer (will need to learn one song confidently ahead of time)

a child to carry the star

If you have a children's choir, there is an opportunity in this liturgy for them to perform a piece or two before the entry of the Kings. I would suggest 'Dona Nobis Pacem'. (Sheet music can be found at <www.music-for-music-teachers.com/dona-nobis-pacem.html> and is free to download.)

Props/costumes

- robes and headscarves for Young Mary and Elder Mary (they should be the same colour);

- robes for the Kings (these can be chasubles);

- gifts for the Kings to bring (they can be found in your vestry! Use a chalice full of gold Christmas tree ornaments, an incense boat, and a pyx);

- a chair;

- a table, with 'peasant'-style props such as earthenware pitchers on it. If you want to be symbolic, you could put out an earthenware goblet and a loaf of bread, to signify the Eucharist;

- a star ornament on a dowel;

- a manger with a baby doll wrapped in swaddling clothes. If you're feeling brave, you can use a real baby, but have a doll on hand in case the baby starts to scream and you have to swap.

You will need to create a 'stage' in the chancel, with the chair and table on it. It is very important that all children have a good view of the stage area, so you may want to consider having chairs or blankets close to the chancel, so younger children can be up front.

The hymn 'A Child is Born in Bethlehem', which is used in the liturgy, is *not* the famous choral piece by Bach. Rather, it is a much less well known Norwegian carol. Amazon has a few versions of this carol – the best one is from *The Christmas Companion, Volume 1* by Garrison Keillor and the cast of *A Prairie Home Companion*. I have altered the lyrics slightly (removing the claim that 'someday angels we shall be' – a common mistake, but human souls do not become angels when we die) and cut a few verses.

I have not been able to find sheet music of this hymn, but this version gives you a clear tune that is easy to learn orally. If you can practise it with the cast, so they know it by the time of the liturgy and can lead the singing, it is very easy for the congregation to sing a cappella. That may seem like a lot of trouble to go to, but it's actually very simple, very memorable, and a wonderful hymn – well worth a few minutes spent in front of a computer learning the tune.

EPIPHANY LITURGY

And we have seen his glory

Reading

Luke 1.46–55

Reader   A reading from the Gospel according to Luke.

Mary said, 'My soul magnifies the Lord,
and my spirit rejoices in God my Saviour,
for he has regarded the low estate of his handmaiden.
For behold, from today all generations will call me blessed;
for he who is mighty has done great things for me, and holy is his name.
And his mercy is on those who fear him from generation to generation.
He has shown strength with his arm,
he has scattered the proud in the imagination of their hearts,
he has put down the mighty from their thrones, and exalted those of low degree;
he has filled the hungry with good things, and the rich he has sent empty away.
He has helped his servant Israel, in remembrance of his mercy,
as he promised to our fathers, to Abraham and to his children for ever.'

Reader returns to seat.

Hymn

Hark! The herald angels sing,
'Glory to the newborn King!
Peace on earth, and mercy mild,
God and sinners reconciled.'
Joyful, all ye nations, rise,
Join the triumph of the skies;
With the angelic host proclaim:
'Christ is born in Bethlehem.'
Hark! The herald angels sing,
'Glory to the newborn King!'

Christ, by highest heav'n adored;
Christ the everlasting Lord!
Late in time behold Him come,
Offspring of a Virgin's womb.
Veiled in flesh the Godhead see;
Hail the incarnate Deity,
Pleased as man with man to dwell,
Jesus, our Emmanuel.
Hark! The herald angels sing,
'Glory to the newborn King!'

(During the last verse of the hymn, ELDER MARY comes up to the chancel.)

> Hail the heav'n-born Prince of Peace!
> Hail the Son of Righteousness!
> Light and life to all He brings,
> Ris'n with healing in His wings.
> Mild He lays His glory by,
> Born that man no more may die,
> Born to raise the sons of earth,
> Born to give them second birth.
> Hark! The herald angels sing,
> 'Glory to the newborn King!'

Elder Mary: Your mothers tell me that you ask to come to my house. I'm flattered. I enjoy having young faces about, people who haven't heard all my stories already, people still ready to wonder at them before taking them apart and fighting over them. I've told you all the ones about the angels, yes? How the angel came to me and told me I was to be the mother of a great king, the King of Kings. You all know that story.

You know how we travelled from Nazareth to Bethlehem and then to Egypt and back home to Nazareth and then into Jerusalem. You know of journeys, and you know the stories you hear from the rabbis, of our people's journeys – Egypt, Babylon – ending always in Jerusalem. We have all travelled many miles, our enemies at our backs or leading us in chains, and we have fought and killed to return.

I saw some of you playing this afternoon with wreaths on your heads that you made out of leaves. Playing kings. You had quite a complicated battle, didn't you? You must be more careful with those sticks; waving them about like that isn't safe. I have had some experience with kings in my time, you know. Perhaps – yes, I think perhaps now is the time for that story. Yes, now, when the thrill of playing at war has not yet gone from your eyes – I will tell you about kings.

And I will tell you of journeys that have a different ending.

Hymn

> O come, all ye faithful, joyful and triumphant,
> O come ye, O come ye, to Bethlehem.
> Come and behold Him, born the King of angels:
>
> > *Refrain:*
> > *O come, let us adore Him,*
> > *O come, let us adore Him,*
> > *O come, let us adore Him,*
> > *Christ the Lord.*
>
> Sing, choirs of angels, sing in exultation;
> Sing, all ye citizens of heaven above!
> Glory to God in the highest:
>
> > *Refrain*

Lo! star-led chieftains, Magi, Christ adoring,
Offer Him incense, gold, and myrrh;
We to the Christ Child bring our hearts' oblations:

> *Refrain*

Yea, Lord, we greet Thee, born this happy morning;
Jesus, to Thee be glory given;
Word of the Father, now in flesh appearing:

> *Refrain*

Elder Mary: Our journey to Bethlehem began as the last stars left the sky, and the sun changed from pink to gold over the horizon. Joseph helped me onto the donkey, and we began plodding down the road. It was empty at first, and cold, but then the sun came up and other people began emptying out of their houses and going to their home towns for the tax. Many of them cursed Rome, and the Roman king, and there was talk of the Messiah coming to free us from Caesar. Of how the Messiah would be born in Bethlehem and save his people from their enemies, how he would lead them on the journey to salvation, and his head would wear the crown of glory for evermore.

And I remembered how the angel had said such things to me. I remembered that the angel had said that the Lord should give my child the throne of his father David. Look around this house – do you see thrones? Do you see royal hangings and attendants as should wait on a king? No – and yet in this house danced the feet of the child King of Kings. This table is where the Lord and Ruler of the world helped me sift the flour into the Sabbath bread. But I'm getting ahead of my story. This house he came to only after a long journey, and it is from this door that he left for a longer and greater one.

Where was I? Yes – people on the road to Bethlehem were talking about the Messiah. And I thought of how God had chosen me, and not an emperor's daughter. And the weight of the child seemed to grow within me, and the road spread out for miles under the donkey's feet, and I wondered why God had chosen a donkey and not a warhorse to carry the unborn King of the World. Why his mother wore a ragged shawl and not a crown. And hearing them talk of the Messiah, of kings and blood and triumph, I wondered what would be the cost I would bear for saying yes to what the angel asked of me. What the cost would be for mothering what the angel had said would be the Prince of Peace.

And I remembered that the old prophecies all spoke of triumph and victory, but not of armies. They spoke of the triumph and victory of peace and justice, the triumph of God, the victory of life. And I knew, as the child almost ready to be born danced inside me, that this was the king I carried, the King of the World, the Lord of Life, and he filled my path with peace.

Hymn

'Peace Is Flowing Like a River' or a children's chorus.

The KINGS enter together from the rear. They sing the following to the tune of 'Ermuntre Dich':

Kings   [*singing*] Break forth, O beauteous heavenly light,
and usher in the morning;

O shepherds, shrink not with affright,
but hear the angel's warning.
This child, now weak in infancy,
our confidence and joy shall be,
the power of Satan breaking,
our peace eternal making.

King 1:   Look, brethren, there is the star – it appears very close now.

King 2:   Did not the Hebrew prophets say that the King of the Jews would be born in Bethlehem?

King 3:   From Bethlehem, for the entire world. From the provinces to the empires. From a mustard seed to the greatest tree of the forest.

King 1:   Let us onward then, to Bethlehem.

King 2:   To seek the King of Kings.

King 3:   To worship the Lord of all.

The Kings move up the aisle and around the church in a figure of eight as they sing. If you like, they can be led by a child holding a candle, or a star ornament. During the hymn, the table onstage is cleared, YOUNG MARY and JOSEPH enter and sit, and the MANGER and BABY JESUS are brought out.

Kings   We three kings of Orient are;
Bearing gifts we traverse afar.
Field and fountain, moor and mountain,
Following yonder star.

Kings and congregation   O star of wonder, star of night,
Star with royal beauty bright,
Westward leading, still proceeding,
Guide us to thy perfect Light.

King 1   Born a king on Bethlehem's plain,
Gold I bring to crown Him again,
King for ever, ceasing never
Over us all to reign.

Kings and congregation   O star of wonder, star of night,
Star with royal beauty bright,
Westward leading, still proceeding,
Guide us to thy perfect Light.

King 2   Frankincense to offer have I.
Incense owns a Deity nigh.
Prayer and praising ever raising,
Worship Him, God on high.

Kings and congregation   O star of wonder, star of night,
Star with royal beauty bright,
Westward leading, still proceeding,
Guide us to thy perfect Light.

King 3   Myrrh is mine: its bitter perfume
Breathes a life of gathering gloom.
Sorrowing, sighing, bleeding, dying,
Sealed in the stone-cold tomb.

Kings and congregation   O star of wonder, star of night,
Star with royal beauty bright,
Westward leading, still proceeding,
Guide us to thy perfect Light.

Glorious now behold Him arise,
King and God and Sacrifice.
Heaven sings Alleluia,
Alleluia the earth replies.

O star of wonder, star of night,
Star with royal beauty bright,
Westward leading, still proceeding,
Guide us to thy perfect Light.

Young Mary   He was born before daybreak, and I wrapped him in bands of cloth, and held him in my arms before laying him down in the manger.

Now the hands of God, the hands that flung forth the stars and called the oceans into being, were curled into fists and punching upwards into the air that smelled of donkey and mouldy hay. God was my son as well as my father, and I saw how helpless he was and how powerless I was to protect him, and I wondered what his journey would hold.

And I wondered what sort of king this was, what sort of God, that could rouse such tenderness in me. Was I not supposed to be the one that God protects? Was God not supposed to rescue me? Was he not my shepherd who would provide for all my needs? So why had I been charged with feeding God, with picking him up when he cried, with teaching him to speak?

Was it not God that gave me life, that gave me my bread, and the words I needed, and comfort? I knew then, as I drifted into sleep, that a sword would pierce my heart also. For God was doing something new.

Hymn

It came upon the midnight clear,
That glorious song of old,
From angels bending near the earth,
To touch their harps of gold;
'Peace on the earth, good will to men,
From Heaven's all gracious King.'
The world in solemn stillness lay,
To hear the angels sing.

Still through the cloven skies they come
With peaceful wings unfurled,

> And still their heavenly music floats
> O'er all the weary world;
> Above its sad and lowly plains,
> They bend on hovering wing,
> And ever o'er its Babel sounds
> The blessèd angels sing.
>
> Yet with the woes of sin and strife
> The world has suffered long;
> Beneath the angel strain have rolled
> Two thousand years of wrong;
> And man, at war with man, hears not
> The love-song which they bring;
> O hush the noise, ye men of strife
> And hear the angels sing.

(During the last verse, the KINGS come onstage and kneel down around the manger.)

> For lo! the days are hastening on,
> By prophet-bards foretold,
> When with the ever circling years
> Comes round the age of gold;
> When peace shall over all the earth
> Her ancient splendours fling,
> And all the world send back the song
> Which now the angels sing.

King 1   Hail, Lord of Life. I am King Melchior, and I bring gold to adorn the King. As gold may be spent or lost or stolen, so do kings pass away.

King 2   Hail, King of Heaven. Hail, Mary, Mother of God. I am King Caspar, and I bring frankincense, to sweeten the world around the King. As the fragrance of incense fills both palace and temple, remember that all earthly power is for the service of God.

King 3   Hail, Alpha and Omega, first and last of all that is. I am King Balthazar, and I bring myrrh, as for a royal burial. As king and peasant alike are returned to dust, remember that God alone is Judge and Lord over all.

King 1   We have read the prophecies of this birth, and we know this child is the King not just of earth but of heaven.

King 2   We have read that his kingdom will be one of justice and peace, and he comes to establish it and bring the reign of God.

King 3   We have read that he is the Messiah, the promised one, for whom the world has waited in bondage. We kings of earth bow before the Eternal Ruler of Heaven, before whom all our kingdoms and our courts are as dust.

Young Mary   Thank you for your gifts and for your kindness.

Hymn (vv. 1 and 2):

A stable-lamp is lighted
Whose glow shall wake the sky;
The stars shall bend their voices,
And every stone shall cry.
And every stone shall cry,
And straw like gold shall shine;
A barn shall harbour heaven,
A stall become a shrine.

This child through David's city
Shall ride in triumph by;
The palm shall strew its branches,
And every stone shall cry.
And every stone shall cry,
Though heavy, dull, and dumb,
And lie within the roadway
To pave His kingdom come.

The KINGS remain in tableau; YOUNG MARY stands and addresses the audience.

Young Mary   God had taken the crowns from the heads of the Kings, and had given them to my little boy, to a dirty little boy whose parents couldn't bribe an innkeeper in a provincial town for a room. God, the King of creation, had made himself a human body, and it was not one that reclined in silks and was attended on comfortably by slaves, but one that cried and wriggled in the cold, that pumped its fists against the indignity of its improvised birth, that sometimes didn't have enough to eat. It was a body whose nose ran in the winter and had only a mother's rough handkerchief to wipe it, a body covered in the scrapes and scratches of a back-street childhood.

God had given himself a voice, a real human voice – you could put your hand to my boy's throat and feel it moving – and it did not speak out from palace balconies or over great armies, but to peasant people in the desert and in the crowded streets of the city, amid the noise and the beggars. That is the kind of royalty that God chose for himself. And he had the whole of history to choose from.

But God's way of making himself King had one thing in common with all the rest. It involved death.

Hymn (vv. 3 and 4)

During the hymn, the KINGS depart. JOSEPH and YOUNG MARY follow them, MARY carrying the child. The manger is cleared away. ELDER MARY comes to centre.

Yet He shall be forsaken,
And yielded up to die;
The sky shall groan and darken,
And every stone shall cry.
And every stone shall cry
For stony hearts of men:

> God's blood upon the spearhead,
> God's love refused again.
>
> But now, as at the ending,
> The low is lifted high;
> The stars shall bend their voices,
> And every stone shall cry.
> And every stone shall cry
> In praises of the child
> By whose descent among us
> The worlds are reconciled.

Elder Mary   You know the story. He went from town to town and he told the good news of God's kingdom. He told them how the kingdom of heaven was like a mustard tree – it begins with the tiniest seed and grows into a tree that all may find rest in.

He frightened the religious leaders, who thought he was going to take away their power. So they killed him. A few politicians, a corrupt priest or two and a fickle crowd, and they killed him.

I stood at the base of the cross, and watched my son suffer, and I stared at the blood on his forehead, and I hated the men who had done this to him – playground bullies, making sport of a boy weaker than they were. And I saw the words written above his head – 'This is the King of the Jews' – and the mocking crown of thorns on his head, and I thought, *This is the end. This is one more journey. One more journey that ends in a crown.* But you know that the story didn't end there.

Hymn

'Of the Father's Heart Begotten' or 'Gabriel's Message Does Away'

Elder Mary   You know that my son's death was not a sacrifice to a bloodthirsty king, that it was not God that required his blood but death itself. You know that God did not kill my son to gain a throne, but rather that in my son God himself died that we might all be crowned with glory.

You know that all his teaching, all his words and stories, came down to one life-giving act, and that all his teaching was to point the way to the cross that leads to heaven. And you have heard the story of how I saw him raised from the dead, the crown of thorns replaced with the crown of life. And how I saw him raised to heaven, to sit at the right hand of God, to be in all places at all times, in our hearts and at our sides and before us on all our journeys.

There is no place in human life where God has not been before us, and there is no place in earth where God is not with us, even now, and to the end of the ages.

Hymn

> A child is born in Bethlehem. Bethlehem.
> Who gladdens all Jerusalem. Halleluiah. Halleluiah.

In a crib, she laid him down.
With joy, the angels gathered round. Halleluiah. Halleluiah.

The Wise Men offered gold and spice,
To welcome him, sweet Jesus Christ. Halleluiah. Halleluiah.

We'll sing his praises without end,
Our brother, Saviour, and our friend. Halleluiah. Halleluiah.

And someday we'll have crowns of gold,
And Jesus' precious face behold. Halleluiah. Halleluiah.

Elder Mary   The crown that was given to him he will give to you. The journey that he has taken –
to death – is one that we all must take, and the path he has made for us brings the
journey's ending from death into life, from darkness into dawn. He has walked this path
before us – he has walked every path before us, and his steps are there to follow, and
he has promised that no matter how hard the road may be, he will not abandon you.
The journey is set, the map is drawn, and at the end of it, for all of you, no matter
how small or poor or helpless – for remember that he was all of those things – there
is a crown.

*At the back of the church, the SOLOIST starts up the aisle, leading JOSEPH, YOUNG MARY, the STAR, the
KINGS and, if you have one, the CHILDREN'S CHOIR, behind her/him. The soloist can sing the first verse
of the hymn, with more and more of the cast joining in the verses as they go along, and the congregation
joining in the chorus. Alternatively, the soloist can sing all four verses by him- or herself, with the cast and
congregation joining in the chorus.*

Hymn

Rev. John D. Matthias
Arranged by Jerome Epstein

91

back was heav-y la-den, his strength was al-most gone; he

shou-ted as he jour-neyed, "De-li-ve-rance will come!"

REFRAIN

Then palms of vic-to-ry, crowns of glo-ry,

palms of vic-to-ry I shall wear.

The summer sun was shining,
The sweat was on his brow,
His garments torn and dusty,
His step was very slow.
He still kept pressing onward
For he was wending home,
And shouted as he journeyed, 'Deliverance will come!'

Refrain:
Then palms of victory, crowns of glory,
Palms of victory I shall wear!

I saw him in the evening,
The sun was bending low,
He overtopped the mountain
And reached the vale below.
He saw that holy city,

His everlasting home,
And shouted loud, 'Hosanna! Deliverance has come!'

Refrain

(At the last verse, the SOLOIST turns and faces the congregation. The cast spreads out over the chancel. The cast and congregation sing the last chorus together.)

While gazing at that city
Across the raging flood,
A band of holy angels
Came from the throne of God.
They bore him on their pinions
Across the raging foam
And joined him in his triumph, 'Deliverance has come!'

Refrain (repeat)

ADDING A EUCHARIST

The obvious place to add a Eucharist to this liturgical pageant would be during the portion that addresses the Passion, somewhere between 'I stood at the base of the cross' and 'You know that my son's death was not a sacrifice to a bloodthirsty king'. However, it would be a challenge to do so without breaking the dramatic tension of that section. So instead, if you want to include a Eucharist, I suggest that you treat what is written as the finale as, instead, the offertory.

- During 'Palms of Victory', the cast processes up from the rear of the church – choose two people to carry up the elements, and, if you wish, encourage the children in the congregation to come and join the cast around the altar.

- If your congregation would be open to the idea, it would be particularly powerful to have the vicar as a cast member, going from playing a part in the drama to performing the Eucharist. For example, your vicar could play Elder Mary, and the Kings could bring the elements up during the offertory, echoing the visual effect of the Kings' presentation of the gifts to the Christ Child. Mary could then remove her headscarf and put on a chasuble, and take her place at the altar to celebrate the Eucharist.

- If you have a male priest with a good singing voice, he could play one of the Kings, and his King costume could be a chasuble – he would then simply remove his crown and take his place at the altar.

- You would then need a closing hymn. 'Lord of the Dance' would be a wonderful choice – providing the same bridge between Christmas and Holy Week as the liturgy does, being a fairly easy one for non-readers to join in, and being quite well known, as well as fun to sing.

ADAPTATIONS FOR SCHOOLS

This is more like a class assembly or play than any of the other liturgies. I would suggest therefore that you look at it as straddling the line of collective worship and a theatrical presentation. One class can prepare it and present it for the others. The whole school can join in on some of the hymns if they have learned them in advance; otherwise, it can be a presentation that happens to be Christian in content, rather than an act of worship.

It would work best presented by Year 5 or 6, as there is quite a lot of reading involved.

- Elder Mary and Young Mary should have music stands for their lines, and their longer speeches can be cut down if necessary – even the best 11-year-old actresses don't have the crowd control of a teenager or adult, and long speeches can make children listening to them restless very easily if they're not done well. However, the cuts should not eliminate the commentary that creates the theme of kingship, as this is central to the message of the piece.

- There are eight roles: Elder Mary, Young Mary, Joseph, three Kings, a Reader and the Star. The rest of the class could do the different singing pieces and make props.

- If you'd like to have more actors, you can use a dozen or so children to act out, silently, what Elder Mary is saying in her speech that begins 'You know the story. He went from town to town …' and discusses Jesus' ministry and death.

EXTENSION ACTIVITIES

Preparation activities

The primary images in the liturgy are those of star, king, journey and crown. The following activities are designed to familiarize children with these images and allow them to explore them creatively, so that they are prepared for the liturgy.

Star of wonder, star of night

The star guided the Kings to Jesus, and stars were used for navigation and by travellers for thousands of years. The constellations guided runaway slaves in America from slavery to freedom – a story whose biblical overtones neatly link Exodus and Passover (travel from slavery to freedom) and the Epiphany story (following the stars to find something that gives you hope).

Read *Follow the Drinking Gourd* with your children. This is an excellent picture book that tells the story of runaway slaves using the stars to help them find their way to freedom.[1] It's available in the UK from several online retailers including Amazon and Foyles.

Follow this by making biscuits in the shape of stars (use the gingerbread recipe in the Christmas chapter and star-shaped cookie cutters) and decorating them. (You can also have a more expressive activity on hand, such as illustrating the song the slaves used, or drawing a map to show the things that happened on their journey, but the biscuits are important for the next part of this activity.)

You can sell the biscuits after church or at a school event and use the money to buy a 'Name A Star' kit. These kits allow you to choose a star and give it a name, receiving a certificate and information about your star (though the name isn't recognized by any astronomical authority). The children can suggest names for your star related to *Follow the Drinking Gourd* or the Epiphany story, or just the name of your church or school, and you can vote on them.

Star with royal beauty bright

Print out maps of the stars and talk about how people used them to travel and find their way in the times before satnav. Show children several different pictures of constellations, and then give them pictures of night skies with stars (a simple Google search of 'night sky with stars' gets you some usable ones) and white coloured pencils or chalk for them to make and name their own constellations.

The light of Christ

The image of the Star of Bethlehem is not just about finding our way to Christ, but also about the light shining in the darkness. The paper lantern activity in the Christmas chapter is therefore appropriate for Epiphany as well.

You could also copy a star shape onto coloured card, and add to each star one of the Bible verses about light listed below. Children who are competent readers could choose their own verse from the list and copy it onto the star. Children can illustrate their chosen verse – you can then cut a hole in the top of the stars and hang them by ribbons throughout the space where the liturgy is to take place.

> And God saw that the light was good; and God separated the light from the darkness.
> (Genesis 1.4)

And the LORD went before them by day in a pillar of cloud to lead them along the way, and by night in a pillar of fire to give them light. (Exodus 13.21)

Yea, thou art my lamp, O LORD, and my God lightens my darkness. (2 Samuel 22.29)

He dawns on them like the morning light, like the sun shining forth upon a cloudless morning, like rain that makes grass to sprout from the earth. (2 Samuel 23.4)

He has redeemed my soul from going down into the Pit, and my life shall see the light. (Job 33.28)

The LORD is my light and my salvation; whom shall I fear? (Psalm 27.1)

He will bring forth your vindication as the light, and your right as the noonday. (Psalm 37.6)

Oh send out thy light and thy truth; let them lead me, let them bring me to thy holy hill and to thy dwelling! (Psalm 43.3)

The people who walked in darkness have seen a great light; those who dwelt in a land of deep darkness, on them has light shined. (Isaiah 9.2)

Arise, shine; for your light has come, and the glory of the LORD has risen upon you. (Isaiah 60.1)

He will bring me forth to the light; I shall behold his deliverance. (Micah 7.9)

Let your light so shine before the people, that they may see your good works and give glory to your Father who is in heaven. (Matthew 5.16)

To give light to those who sit in darkness and in the shadow of death, and to guide our feet into the way of peace. (Luke 1.79)

The light shines in the darkness, and the darkness has not overcome it. (John 1.5)

Again Jesus spoke to them, saying, 'I am the light of the world; he who follows me will not walk in darkness, but will have the light of life.' (John 8.12)

The night is far gone, the day is at hand. Let us then cast off the works of darkness and put on the armour of light. (Romans 13.12)

For once you were darkness, but now you are light in the Lord; walk as children of light. (Ephesians 5.8)

But if we walk in the light, as he is in the light, we have fellowship with one another, and the blood of Jesus his Son cleanses us from all sin. (1 John 1.7)

Crowns of glory

Children can make and decorate their own crowns (as mentioned in the All Saints/All Souls chapter). Hope Education has a class headdress-making set that comes with crowns to cut out and lots of decorations. You should also have paint or felt tips available so children can draw on their crowns if they want. They can then bring their crowns to the liturgy and put them on when Mary says 'The crown that was given to him will be given to you.'

The king in the stable

Local homelessness charities are usually receptive to donations of toiletries and household items. Your children can design posters to hang around the church or school, reminding people to bring in these items. At the liturgy, place a basket by the door of the church and place a crib scene on a table next to it. As people come in to the liturgy, they can leave their donations in the basket, next to the image of the Christ Child in his 'temporary accommodation'.

Journey to Bethlehem

This is similar to the scavenger hunt in the Christmas chapter, but more structured – and therefore requiring more preparation. But I have fond childhood memories of similar activities – it's worth the effort.

This is a treasure hunt, with clues, that leads the children, like the Kings, to find the Christ Child. The clues are on page 99 – you can photocopy them and print them out.

It follows the story of God's people through their struggles in the Old Testament to God's promise of the Saviour. Each clue should be hidden along with a Christmas tree ornament that goes along with that story. When the children finally find the Christ Child, they can bring him and all the clues to the manger scene and hang the ornaments on your church's Christmas tree. Place the clues as follows:

1 Children start with Clue 1 in hand.

2 Clue 2 is hidden in the church garden. If you don't have a garden, hide it by the flowers at the altar.

3 Clue 3 should be hidden by a stained-glass window or kneeler that has a picture of Noah's Ark on it. If you have a Noah's Ark toy in one of your Sunday School spaces, you could also hide it there.

4 Clue 4 is hidden by the font.

5 Clue 5 is hidden by the altar.

6 Clue 6 is hidden somewhere dark and far away from the main part of the church, like the narthex or a stairwell or basement.

7 The Christ Child figure is hidden by a cross.

Processing activities

If you weren't able to have one after your Christmas liturgy, this would be a good time to have a final Christmas party. If you have had a Christmas party already, here are some other ideas for following up this liturgy.

At the end of your Epiphany celebration, whatever form it takes, I suggest giving children a gift – the Three Kings from the liturgy could even hand them out. Gold chocolate coins are a good one – they look like the gold that the Kings gave to Jesus, they're budget friendly, and they're delicious!

Kinaesthetic

In a self-contained area (perhaps a large tabletop, a 'Pray and Play' area or the chancel of a chapel), set up a crib scene, along with a variety of other materials. These should include such items as blocks, toy trees, fabric in different plain colours, rocks, sand, potted plants, Godly Play or Playmobil figures, toy animals in the same scale as the people, and cardboard boxes/wooden stools that can be covered with cloth and turned into mountains, and whatever else your imagination can come up with.

With the children, set up a model of the Kings' journey. Worry less about historical accuracy than about imagination – what obstacles might they have faced? What would they need on their journey?

Creative

The star is a symbol of the light shining in darkness, and in winter this is particularly appropriate. Many companies make pens that can draw on glass (Google search for 'glass pens') – children can use them to decorate glass candle-holders, or draw on square pieces of glass to make stained-glass windows. The light shining through the window, or the candle in the holder, will be like the star, shining in darkness to show the way to the Christ Child.

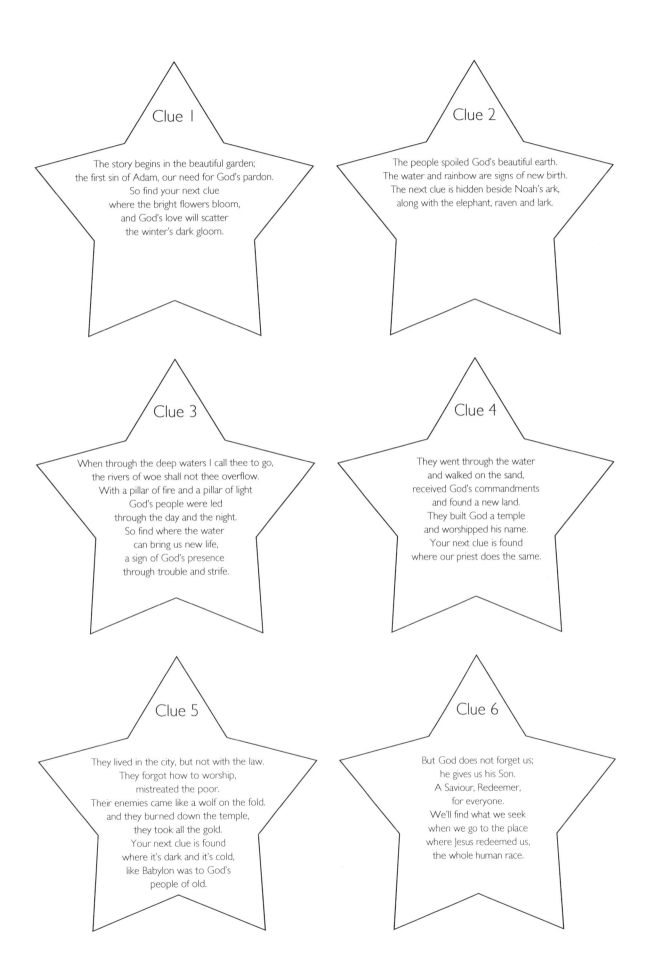

Clue 1

The story begins in the beautiful garden;
the first sin of Adam, our need for God's pardon.
So find your next clue
where the bright flowers bloom,
and God's love will scatter
the winter's dark gloom.

Clue 2

The people spoiled God's beautiful earth.
The water and rainbow are signs of new birth.
The next clue is hidden beside Noah's ark,
along with the elephant, raven and lark.

Clue 3

When through the deep waters I call thee to go,
the rivers of woe shall not thee overflow.
With a pillar of fire and a pillar of light
God's people were led
through the day and the night.
So find where the water
can bring us new life,
a sign of God's presence
through trouble and strife.

Clue 4

They went through the water
and walked on the sand,
received God's commandments
and found a new land.
They built God a temple
and worshipped his name.
Your next clue is found
where our priest does the same.

Clue 5

They lived in the city, but not with the law.
They forgot how to worship,
mistreated the poor.
Their enemies came like a wolf on the fold.
and they burned down the temple,
they took all the gold.
Your next clue is found
where it's dark and it's cold,
like Babylon was to God's
people of old.

Clue 6

But God does not forget us;
he gives us his Son.
A Saviour, Redeemer,
for everyone.
We'll find what we seek
when we go to the place
where Jesus redeemed us,
the whole human race.

Verbal

Italian folklore has a wonderful story about 'Old Befana', the Christmas witch. In the story, Befana is an elderly woman who is sweeping her step when the Three Kings come by and ask for directions to the Christ Child, and invite her to come with them on their search. Too busy with her housekeeping, she declines. However, she changes her mind after they have left, and sets off with gifts to find the Christ Child. She never finds him, and has spent all the centuries since searching for him. But since any child she sees might be the Christ Child, she leaves gifts for all children at Epiphany.

Read a retelling of the Befana story (Tomie de Paola's is wonderful) and encourage children to rewrite the story imagining they are Befana or one of the Three Kings. This would make a good Sunday School session for the Sunday after Epiphany, if the liturgy was held on the day of Epiphany itself. If the children are coming directly from a liturgy into this activity, that may be taxing the attention span of even the most patient child.

Multi-sensory

An Epiphany sense table could include the following:

- *sight*: A bowl full of gold Christmas tree ornaments, a variety of crib scenes from different cultures (wooden or fabric, so they can be played with).

- *smell/touch*: Frankincense and myrrh. These can be bought fairly cheaply and easily from Amazon.

- *taste*: Many countries, including England, have an Epiphany tradition in which a coin (or a bean or a small king figure) is hidden inside a cake, and whoever gets the slice with the coin in it is king or queen for the day. If you don't have time to bake a cake, you can buy un-iced fairy cakes, stick a coin in one of them, and then ice them all to disguise which one has the coin. Each child who comes to the table is given a fairy cake to eat and told to eat *carefully*! (It's probably best to limit this activity to children aged five and over and to use a large 2p or £2 coin, or else a small bean, to prevent any risk of choking. If you have younger children present, you can provide a separate set of fairy cakes for them, none of which has a coin in it.) Whoever finds the coin or bean is given a crown and three cheers.

- *hearing*: Putomayo's *Christmas Around the World* CD[2] includes some Christmas music that may be less familiar to children than our regular stable of carols.

EXTENSIONS FOR HOME

In many parts of the world, children receive their gifts at Epiphany, rather than Christmas. You might hold back some presents from Christmas morning, and give them on Epiphany instead. This reminds your children that Christmas lasts for 12 whole days – it doesn't end on 25 December. (This also has the salutary effect of minimizing the Boxing Day letdown, and the tantrums and whining that can often accompany it, as well as allowing you to get some Christmas presents in the sales!)

In many Spanish-speaking countries, children leave their shoes by the doors of their rooms on the night of 5 January. The next morning, they find that the 'Three Kings' have visited in the night and left them presents!

In English folklore, the night before Epiphany is 'Twelfth Night', the last day of the feast of misrule. On Twelfth Night, kings would dress up as peasants and peasants as kings. There would be wassailing (going from door to door and singing raucous songs in exchange for food or money, as well as singing to the trees and crops that would give you your harvest) and mummers' plays.

You can have a Twelfth Night festival at home. Let your children be parents for the day – seat them in your regular places at the dinner table, let them dress up in your clothes, and allow them to boss you around and dictate table manners. (In exchange, you can dress up as children and have fun eating with your fingers, talking with your mouth full, and so on, making your children tell you off for it!)

Another Twelfth Night tradition was the mummers' play – a skit that retold the legends of English folklore, often with a dose of irreverent humour. If you have children who love to put on plays, suggest that they spend the day putting together a Three Kings' Day play and present it after dinner.

You can also read them the story of Befana (or, in Russian folklore, Babushka), the 'Christmas witch' mentioned in the previous section. This is a more melancholy story, and would create less of a festival feeling, but it does have a very profound lesson at its heart – not to be so distracted by the trivia of daily life that you forget to seek the transcendent. I would suggest, however, that you avoid pointing out the moral to your children – let them encounter the story unhindered by adult interpretations, and come to make their own meaning from it.

Twelfth Night may also be a good time for family trips. Many people have an annual trip to the theatre or the ballet for offerings such as *The Nutcracker*. Why not wait until Epiphany? Many runs continue into January, and if you save your trip for Twelfth Night you will have one less thing to do in the run-up to Christmas, you will be battling smaller crowds, and you will be teaching your children that Christmas continues for 12 whole days, and that we celebrate it, as Christians, in its entirety.

ASH WEDNESDAY

Behold, I make all things new

INTRODUCTION

There is an understandable reluctance among many Sunday School and RE leaders to discuss sin with children. We want our children to feel a strong sense of self, to feel positive about themselves, and to believe in a God who loves and accepts them for who they are.

But you cannot have Christianity without sin; the world calls out to God in pain, ridden with selfishness, greed, fear, cruelty and war, and God responds by becoming one of us and saving us from that sin and giving us life that lasts for ever. This is the good news we have to present to children, and it is richer and more meaningful than a recitation of 'I'm OK, you're OK.' And if our children are to share in the joy of Easter, they must share in the sorrow of Lent. As Richard Chartres, Bishop of London, has pointed out, if we do not allow for the troughs in the year, we do not experience the peaks; instead, we have a constant dull monotone, an attempt at continuous carnival that cannot be sustained.[1] Lent allows our children to enter the most sacred places with us, and to emerge at Easter renewed, reborn and rejoicing.

The Ash Wednesday liturgy encourages children to reflect on sin both individual and communal. They are asked to choose, on their own, one thing about themselves they would like to change; this action, and that of literally sending their old habits up in smoke, means that their contemplation of sin is personal, between themselves and God, and free from adult interference. The intercessions also reflect on the sins of humanity as a whole, encouraging children to consider how Christianity may be applied to the outside world. The emphasis, reflected in the closing hymn, is on the idea that we are all broken human beings, struggling through life together, with our hope set on the promise of Christ's incarnation and resurrection. It reminds us that Lent is a time of purification, of paring our lives down to their essentials, free from the clutter that muffles the voice of God.

I have done this liturgy at night during a lock-in, and its imagery of light and darkness works very well in that setting.

I use 'Palms of Victory' in this liturgy as well as the one for Epiphany. This is deliberate, as the theme of journey and struggle is common to both services. The repetition of hymns, prayers and Bible readings at different times of the year can help children make connections between the themes of the two festivals.

SET-UP AND PREPARATION

1 Chairs in a semi-circle around the altar. Place a piece of paper and a pen on each chair. You may choose on this occasion to place the orders of service on the chairs in advance as well, to

provide fewer distractions as the children enter. That may enhance the simple, meditative atmosphere that is so important for Lent.

2 Most of the church should be in darkness. If you have a large cross in your chancel, illuminate it, and make sure there are enough lights on so that the children don't trip and can see their hymn sheets. Apart from that, the church should be as dark as possible.

3 You may wish to have incense burning, or use scented candles on the altar.

4 In front of the altar, there should be a purple cloth. On this, place one large candle, a large bowl, long tapers, and enough tealights in holders for each child to have one.

5 If you are not using live musicians, you will need a CD player or docked iPod with 'Palms of Victory', a quiet instrumental piece of your choice, and Leonard Cohen's 'Hallelujah' on it. (I've cut the sexually explicit verse from 'Hallelujah', as well as a few others. You can download a karaoke version of this song, in which case it doesn't matter how many verses you have or what order they're in. Alternatively, you can sing it a cappella – it's pretty easy if you have one confident leader.) You will also need music playing while the children are writing or drawing what they're giving up for Lent – I suggest 'Ashokan Farewell', a beautiful piece for violin and piano that creates a contemplative mood. It is available for download on <www.emusic.co.uk> and Amazon.

6 Any resources you need for telling the story of Jesus' temptation. I have provided a script for the telling of the temptation story, but if you would prefer to use another storytelling method, you can substitute your own.

7 As always, a fire extinguisher. You never know.

If your children don't know the songs, it may help to have the leader sing the verses and the children join in on the choruses, both of which are easily learned. If you don't have someone to accompany 'Palms of Victory' using the sheet music, you can download it and the congregation can sing along. It is available for download on Amazon – search 'Revels Palms of Victory'.

I have given within the text of the liturgy the wondering questions we used – feel free to change or adapt them for your own congregation.

ASH WEDNESDAY LITURGY

Behold, I make all things new

We enter the church in silence. We sit in chairs in a semi-circle around the altar.

Leader   O God, make speed to save us.

All   **O Lord, make haste to help us.**

Reading

Isaiah 53.3–6

Reader   A reading from the book of the prophet Isaiah.

He was despised and rejected by men; a man of sorrows, and acquainted with grief; and as one from whom men hide their faces he was despised, and we esteemed him not.

Surely he has borne our griefs and carried our sorrows; yet we esteemed him stricken, smitten by God, and afflicted.

But he was wounded for our transgressions, he was bruised for our iniquities; upon him was the chastisement that made us whole, and with his stripes we are healed.

All we like sheep have gone astray; we have turned every one to his own way; and the LORD has laid on him the iniquity of us all.

All   **Holy God,**
Holy and Mighty,
Holy Immortal One,
have mercy on us.

Leader   After Jesus was baptized, he spent forty days in the wilderness. During the season of Lent, Christians all over the world follow the example of Jesus, and spend forty days in penitence and fasting, remembering the promise of God's forgiveness and love shown at Easter.

Together, therefore, let us go with Jesus into the desert. Let us observe this holy season of Lent together. Let us each give up something, so that we may live a simpler life, growing closer to God.

And let us begin by remembering our sins, those times when we have not lived up to what God has made us to be.

Let us pray to God.

For the times we have been selfish, thoughtless or cruel.
Holy God,

All   **Holy and Mighty,**
Holy Immortal One,
have mercy upon us.

Leader   For the times when we have not been grateful for the gifts you have given us.
Holy God,

**All   Holy and Mighty,
Holy Immortal One,
have mercy upon us.**

Leader   By your love for us in creation and your faithfulness when we turn away from you,
Holy God,

**All   Holy and Mighty,
Holy Immortal One,
have mercy upon us.**

Leader   By your incarnation and teaching, your death and resurrection,
Holy God,

**All   Holy and Mighty,
Holy Immortal One,
have mercy upon us.**

Leader   In our sleeping and our waking, in our joys and sorrows, our death and our life,
Holy God,

**All   Holy and Mighty,
Holy Immortal One,
have mercy upon us.**

Silence is kept.

Hymn

Pre- cious Lord take my hand, lead me on Let me stand, I am tired. I am

weak, I am worn. Through the storm, Through the night, Lead me on, To the

light, Take my hand pre- cious Lord And lead me on, (Lead me on)

Story: The temptation of Christ

Reader   When Jesus was grown up,
He went down to the River Jordan.
His cousin, John the Baptist, was there,
With lots of people.

John was baptizing the people.
He brought them into the water and said,
'Repent of your sins and God will forgive you!'

Jesus went down to the river,
And John baptized him.
He poured the water over Jesus' head,
And a voice came down from heaven, saying,
'This is my beloved Son – listen to him.'

Jesus knew that God had chosen him
To do God's work among the people.
To tell them about God,
To heal the sick,
To give sight to the blind,
And to raise the dead.

But before he went out to do his work.
He went all by himself, into the desert,
To be all alone with God.
He fasted for forty days and forty nights,
Not eating or drinking.

And there, the Evil One came to him.

'If you really *are* God's son,
The Chosen One,
The Messiah,' the Evil one said,
'Turn these stones into bread.
You must be *really hungry*.
If you really *are* the Messiah, you can do it.'

Jesus said, 'It is written in Scripture,
"Man does not live by bread alone,
But by the word of God".'

And the Evil One went away.
But then he came back.

'If you really *are* God's son,
The Chosen One,
The Messiah,' the Evil One said,
'Prove it to everyone.
Jump off the top of the temple in Jerusalem.
Doesn't it say in Scripture

That God will send angels to catch you?
Think about it – *everyone* will believe in you.
You'll have power. You'll be important.'

But Jesus said, 'It is written in Scripture,
"You shall not put God to the test".'

And the Evil One went away.
But then he came back.

And he took Jesus to a high mountain.
And showed him all the kingdoms of the world
And the glory of them.
And he said,
'I will give you all of this
If you will fall down and worship me.'

But Jesus said, 'Get behind me, Satan!
For it is written in Scripture, "Worship only God".'

And the Evil One went away,
And angels came and ministered to Jesus.

When the reading is over, we wonder about the story.

Leader   I wonder what your favourite part of the story was.
I wonder what the most important part of the story was.
I wonder what it would feel like to be all alone with God.
I wonder how Jesus felt when the Evil One talked to him.
I wonder what stopped him doing what the Evil One wanted.

Hymn

Rev. John D. Matthias
Arranged by Jerome Epstein

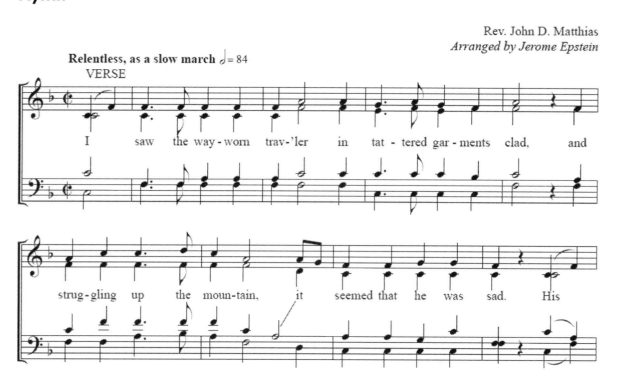

Relentless, as a slow march ♩ = 84
VERSE

I saw the way-worn trav-'ler in tat-tered gar-ments clad, and

strug-gling up the moun-tain, it seemed that he was sad. His

back was heav-y la-den, his strength was al-most gone; he

shou-ted as he jour-neyed, "De - li - ve-rance will come!"

REFRAIN

Then palms of vic-to-ry, crowns of glo-ry,

palms of vic-to-ry I shall wear.

The summer sun was shining,
The sweat was on his brow,
His garments torn and dusty,
His step was very slow.
He still kept pressing onward
For he was wending home,
And shouted as he journeyed, 'Deliverance will come!'

Refrain: Then palms of victory, crowns of glory,
Palms of victory I shall wear!

I saw him in the evening,
The sun was bending low,
He overtopped the mountain
And reached the vale below.
He saw that holy city,
His everlasting home,

And shouted loud, 'Hosanna! Deliverance has come!'

Refrain

While gazing at that city,
Across the raging flood
A band of holy angels
Came from the throne of God.
They bore him on their pinions
Across the raging foam
And joined him in his triumph, 'Deliverance has come!'

Refrain

Leader   Please take a moment to think about some of the things you may want to give up for Lent.

We are silent for a moment. You may want to give up a bad habit, like teasing your brothers or sisters. You may want to give up something like playing too much PlayStation or watching too much TV. You may want to give up something like sweets, to help yourself live more simply and resist temptation. You may want to give up spending all your pocket money on yourself and start giving some of it to charity.

Leader   I wonder if anyone would like to share what they are giving up for Lent.

When a few people have shared, the leader says:

Leader   I invite you now to write, or draw, what you are giving up for Lent on your piece of paper. When you have finished, come up one by one and I will help you set your paper alight with the candle, placing it to burn to ashes in the bowl. In this way, we will see our bad habits, and the things that keep us from being our best selves, go up in smoke, and be made new.

As we write or draw on our papers, quiet music plays.

When everything has been burnt, the leader takes the bowl of ashes and distributes them to the children, making the sign of the cross in ashes on our foreheads.

Leader   Remember that you are dust, and to dust you shall return.

When we have received our ashes, we light a little candle from the big candle and place it on the altar.

Reading

Revelation 21.1–4b

Reader   A reading from the book of Revelation.

Then I saw a new heaven and a new earth; for the first heaven and the first earth had passed away, and the sea was no more. And I saw the holy city, new Jerusalem, coming down out of heaven from God, prepared as a bride adorned for her husband; and I heard a loud voice from the throne saying, 'Behold, the dwelling of God is with people. He will dwell with them, and they shall be his people, and God himself will be with them; he will wipe away every tear from their eyes, and death shall be no more, neither shall there be mourning nor crying nor pain any more, for the former things have passed away.' And he who sat upon the throne said, 'Behold, I make all things new.'

Song

I've heard there was a secret chord
That David played, and it pleased the Lord
But you don't really care for music, do you?
It goes like this – the fourth, the fifth
The minor fall, the major lift
The baffled king composing Hallelujah

Hallelujah, Hallelujah
Hallelujah, Hallelujah

Maybe I've been here before
I know this room, I've walked this floor
I used to live alone before I knew you.
But I've seen your flag on the marble arch
And love is not a victory march
It's a cold and it's a broken Hallelujah

Hallelujah, Hallelujah
Hallelujah, Hallelujah

Maybe there's a God above
And all I've ever learned from love
Was how to shoot at someone who outdrew you
It's not a cry you can hear at night
It's not somebody who has seen the light
It's a cold and it's a broken Hallelujah

Hallelujah, Hallelujah
Hallelujah, Hallelujah

I did my best, it wasn't much
I couldn't feel, so I tried to touch
I've told the truth, I didn't come to fool you
And even though it all went wrong
I'll stand before the Lord of Song
With nothing on my tongue but Hallelujah

Hallelujah, Hallelujah
Hallelujah, Hallelujah

As we leave church, we pass by the font, which is filled with water. If you want, you can rub the ash cross off your forehead, or it can remain as you go into the world.

ADDING A EUCHARIST

The best place for a Eucharist in this service is between the imposition of ashes and the reading from Revelation. The Eucharist then serves as the act that makes the bridge from atonement (imposition of ashes) to redemption ('Behold, I make all things new'). The children are already gathered around the altar, and the atmosphere is quiet and reverential, so there is no need to add an offertory. Two children can simply bring the elements from a side table to the altar while the last few ashes are being imposed; the children are then invited to stand and begin the eucharistic prayer.

The tactile lyrics of 'Hallelujah' become much more potent when they follow communion – from 'I couldn't feel, so I tried to touch' to 'with nothing on my tongue but Hallelujah'.

ADAPTATIONS FOR SCHOOLS

As there is no movement between different spaces in this liturgy, it is easier than some of the others to adapt for a school environment. The challenge here is in the interactive element of the service – the burning of sins and the imposition of ashes made from those sins.

There is a way of doing this with a large group that preserves the symbolism of having the ashes for the children's forehead literally made out of their own frailties, but it requires sensibly behaved children. You will also need adult helpers, a large fireproof bucket and matches instead of a large candle, and several bowls.

- At the beginning of the service, the adults should stand by the door with paper and pens, handing them to the children as they come in. At the point in the service when the children have written down the thing they are letting go of this Lent, they should pass their pieces of paper along their row and hand them to the adults (make sure the children fold them tightly, so others in their row can't see what's been written). Place all the sins in the bucket and light them with the matches (this will be similar, image-wise, to the lighting of the new fire at the Easter Vigil). Have a fire extinguisher on hand, and some backup ashes.

- Instead of immediately going to the imposition of ashes, allow the fire to burn while you move on to the final reading and the singing of 'Hallelujah'. During the singing of 'Hallelujah', hand to each adult helper a portion of the ashes in his or her own bowl. Position the adults at each door out of the hall/church, and play 'Ashokan Farewell' again as the pupils leave. As each pupil passes an adult, the adult makes the ash cross on the pupil's forehead and says the words, 'Remember that you are dust, and to dust you shall return.'

For more difficult children (and more risk-averse head teachers), I suggest the following:

- Instead of the bucket, have four or five pots of soil, and some seeds, ready at the front. Have pre-made ashes on hand, already divided into several bowls. Use adult helpers in the same way as above to pass out pens and paper to each child as they come in, and to collect the children's 'sins'.

- Instead of burning them, bury the sins, and then choose children to come and plant seeds. Explain that the paper the 'sins' are written on will break down and decay, turning into new life just as the sinful parts of ourselves can be broken down and turned into new life through the redemption of Jesus.

- The children can then come up a row at a time to have ashes imposed, with adults standing at several stations at the front of the hall or church, so five or six children can receive their ashes at once (play music while this is happening). Alternatively, you can impose the ashes as described above, as the children are dismissed.

- If you impose the ashes during the service instead of at the dismissal, adults can be ready with bowls of water and cloths at the doors as the pupils leave, if they want to have their ash cross symbolically baptized away as they depart.

EXTENSION ACTIVITIES

Unlike many other festivals, Ash Wednesday is not easily transferred to the nearest weekend, so an extended church celebration on the day itself is almost impossible. In fact, you're lucky if any children come to church at all – I've carried out the liturgy above on the first Saturday of Lent instead, as part of a sleepover. But there should be *some* marking of the entry into Lent with your children, even if it isn't on Ash Wednesday itself.

Preparation activities

The celebration of the start of Lent really begins the day before Ash Wednesday, on Shrove Tuesday, known to modern secular society as Pancake Day. Therefore, the best preparation activity for the Ash Wednesday liturgy is the marking of Shrove Tuesday.

As a result of the Reformation, British society has lost its carnival spirit in the build-up to Lent, but in medieval times, the end of the season of Epiphany was a time for feasting, celebration, the reversal of power structures, and general chaos and upheaval. This is still the tradition in many countries – from Germany to Brazil, the carnival season is celebrated with costumes, parades, all-night dance parties, and the great old custom of eating your weight in buttered foodstuffs. The word 'carnival' itself is thought to derive from the Latin *carne vale*, or 'farewell to meat' (the traditional Lenten discipline involved giving up meat). The joy of Christmas is not supposed to go gently into the good night of Lent. We are facing 40 days of deprivation, austerity, and self-sacrifice – before that comes, let's party!

Your Shrove Tuesday party should, ideally, be a celebration with the whole church, not just the children. Here are some suggestions for making it go with a swing:

Ideas for food

Pancakes

This one almost goes without saying, but it can be made even more decadent (and easy on the cooks) if the cooks produce plain pancakes and a table nearby is *packed* with toppings, from Nutella to strawberry jam to banana slices to sugar to lemon juice ... let people top their own, and second helpings are encouraged!

Ice cream sundaes

Again, a topping station is a good idea. And include as many flavours as possible.

King cake

The tradition mentioned in the Epiphany chapter, of having a cake with a coin hidden in it, is also used in many places on Shrove Tuesday. Whoever gets the slice with the coin is the king or queen of the carnival.

Ideas for entertainment

A pantomime

Write or buy a short pantomime script, collect a few costume pieces, and cast and perform it on the day for maximum silliness. The carnival feel is what's wanted here – you can even hand out noisemakers to the audience and include some audience participation in the singing. If you're lucky, a male vicar or churchwarden will volunteer to be the dame.

Pub quiz

Include three or four child-friendly questions in each round, so everyone can participate. Make sure each team has a suitably silly name, and include booby prizes for the worst performers (bonus points to you if the vicar's team comes last).

Talent show

This is how the church I grew up in celebrated Shrove Tuesday. The choir did some silly piece (P.D.Q. Bach was popular), and parishioners prepared short skits at home, many of which were re-creations of famous sketches. Get the churchwardens to do the dead parrot sketch, and if you can end the evening with your vicar slouched in a chair asking 'Does my face look bovvered?' you can count the night a success.

I realize these ideas make this sound like the official 'humiliate the vicar' party, but that's not intentional. Honestly. All right, maybe it is. But that's what makes it fun!

Processing activities

The beginning of Lent itself is probably best celebrated with children on the first Saturday or Sunday of Lent. You can adapt the liturgy in this chapter to be a Sunday School session, with the water in a (nice) bowl by the door rather than in the font. Here are some activities which will supplement the themes and imagery found in the liturgy.

Hiding the Alleluia

I have tried to research the origins of this tradition, and failed, so I will say only that it did not come from me, and that it has been around for at least 20 years.

During Lent, we don't say the word 'Alleluia'. In fact, the inclusion of the song 'Hallelujah' in my Ash Wednesday liturgy is deeply subversive, and intended to evoke a feeling of commingled light and darkness – as John Chrysostom once wrote, 'Weeping over the grave we make our song; Alleluia, Alleluia, Alleluia.' On the edges of Lent, rejoicing breaks through, before we plummet into its depths. Introducing a few Alleluias into Good Friday would be a nice bracketing of this idea.

But in general, we don't say 'Alleluia' in Lent. This is because Lent is a time of sober reflection, and 'Alleluia' is a cry of joy. For the same reason we don't sing the Gloria in Lent. We have put aside the trappings of rejoicing and put on the sackcloth of penitence. All these pent-up Alleluias will come bursting out at high volume at the Easter Vigil (that is, if you do it right!), and will have been made more joyful and raucous by their lengthy suppression through the 40 days.

Children can be involved in hiding the Alleluia by making a banner (or a set of eight single-lettered A3 posters) saying 'ALLELUIA' at the start of Lent. There should be no decoration on the word whatsoever – no borders, no fancy backgrounds. In the presence of the congregation, the children hide the Alleluia out of sight, preferably under the altar.

Sometime during Lent – not at a service, but in secret, during a children's programme or a Sunday School session, the Alleluia is spirited out of the altar and decorated. Play up the subterfuge of this exercise. Tell the children, 'Sshhh, don't tell the adults what we're doing – let it be a surprise!'

Figure 7 *Alleluia banner*

and repeatedly remind them, 'DON'T SAY THIS WORD. I don't want *anyone* to say this word until Easter. It is LENT. We *do not say this word!!*' They will love it, I promise.

After it's decorated – with symbols of spring and Easter, such as crosses, eggs, rising suns, flowers, butterflies, rabbits, angels, trees, an empty tomb, etc. – it goes back into hiding. On Easter morning, the children take it out of its hiding place and reveal it – transformed and bursting with life! – to the congregation.

Ours becomes part of the altar decoration on Easter Sunday, and is then carried in procession to the square where we hold our Easter egg hunt, but yours can be hung in your Easter garden or over a gallery, or even placed by the door of the church. You can make your Alleluia whatever size and shape you need to fulfil its role. To hang it, you just need to fold over and hem the top and insert a dowel through the loop. Then attach screw eyes to each side of the dowel and tie ribbon around the screw eyes. You can then hang the ribbon by a cup hook. If you use your banner as an altar frontal, all you need are heavy candlesticks on the altar to hold it down at each corner.

Charity projects

The Lenten calendar in the 'Extensions for home' section can be used as a Sunday School project as well as an individual family project. Children can decorate money boxes at the beginning of Lent (Baker Ross makes cardboard ones) and take them, and a calendar, home. The children collect the money throughout Lent, and bring the boxes in on Easter Sunday, when they are gathered in at the altar at the offertory.

EXTENSIONS FOR HOME

Preparing the home for Lent

Together, you can ritually prepare your house for Lent by removing any palm crosses you have and bringing them to church, getting rid of things that you feel are keeping you away from God (too many video games? Too much cake and self-indulgence?), and, if you feel inclined, covering any crosses in your home with purple cloth.

A Lenten calendar

Advent calendars are standard, but what is there to help a child count down the 40 days of Lent?

Children may enjoy making their own Lenten calendar, and this can be a good way of exploring the imagery of Lent and Easter.

You can make a Lenten calendar out of card or felt. Begin by taking one large piece of card or felt (A3 or larger) for the background. Use another piece of paper or felt to make the pockets – cut from it 40 small squares approximately equal in size, one for each pocket. Glue three edges of each square and stick them to the background with the unglued edge uppermost, creating a pocket. Make a row of four squares at the top, and below this six rows of six squares. Label the squares of each six-square column with the day of the week, from Monday to Saturday. Label the top row from Wednesday to Saturday.

Sundays are not included, as Sundays are considered to be in Lent, but not of Lent – all Sundays are feasts of the Resurrection, and therefore it is forbidden to fast on them. You are allowed – no, *commanded* – to break your Lenten fast on every Lenten Sunday.

If you don't take my word for it, do the maths. Six weeks of seven days each, plus the five days from Ash Wednesday to the first Sunday of Lent, minus Easter Sunday itself, equals ... 46 days. Take away the six Sundays, and you have the 40 days of Lent.

Now decorate each square with a symbol of Lent. If you're skilled enough in theology to come up with 40 separate symbols of Lent, I applaud you. However, I would suggest either having a different symbol for each week (copying it six times, or four times for week one, so you still have one for each pocket), or a different symbol for each day of the week (again, copying each six times, or seven for Wednesday to Saturday). These can each have a prayer or a Bible verse on the back of them. If your Lenten calendar is small, you could put only the reference on the back, and look up the verse.

The table on page 118 shows a suggested scheme, but you can come up with your own. This one is based on the seven 'I am' statements in the Gospel of John.

Here are some other symbols you can use:

- *Fish*: John 6 – loaves and fishes. Also, the fish as a symbol for Jesus, derived from the Greek ICHTHUS, which means fish, and consists of the first letters of each of the Greek words 'Jesus Christ, son of God, Saviour'.

- *Wheat*: John 12.24 – '... unless a grain of wheat falls into the earth and dies, it remains alone; but if it dies, it bears much fruit.'

A Lenten calendar		
Week 1 (Ash Wednesday to 1st Saturday)	**Symbol**: Bread	**Bible verse:** John 6.35: Then Jesus declared, 'I am the bread of life. He who comes to me will never go hungry, and he who believes in me will never be thirsty.'
Week 2	**Symbol**: Candle	**Bible verse:** John 8.12: Again Jesus spoke to [the people] saying, 'I am the light of the world. Whoever follows me will never walk in darkness, but will have the light of life.'
Week 3	**Symbol**: Door	**Bible verse:** John 10.7: So again Jesus said, 'Truly, truly, I tell you, I am the gate for the sheep.'
Week 4	**Symbol**: Shepherd	**Bible verse:** John 10.11: 'I am the good shepherd. The good shepherd lays down his life for the sheep.'
Week 5	**Symbol**: Empty tomb	**Bible verse:** John 11.25: Jesus said to her, 'I am the resurrection and the life; he who believes in me though he die, yet shall he live.'
Week 6	**Symbol**: Path	**Bible verse:** John 14.6: Jesus answered, 'I am the way and the truth and the life. No one comes to the Father except through me.'
Week 7 – Holy Week	**Symbol**: Vine	**Bible verse:** John 15.1, 5: 'I am the true vine, and my Father is the vine-grower. I am the vine; you are the branches.'

- *Fire*: Daniel 3.1–27 – the Israelites in the fiery furnace, or Exodus 3.1–10 – the burning bush.

- *Dove/bird*: John 1.32 – Jesus anointed by the dove at his baptism, or Matthew 23.37–38 – Jesus laments over Jerusalem.

- *Lamb*: Exodus 12.1–13 – commandment to the Israelites about the Passover lamb.

- *Water*: Exodus 14.10–22 – delivery at the Red Sea.

- *Grapes*: Mark 12.1–9 – the parable of the vineyard, or Mark 14.23–24 – the institution of the Eucharist.

These have longer Bible references, as they often show the symbol being used in the context of the whole story. It might be interesting, with older children, to compare the use of the symbol in two different places in the Bible, so I have sometimes used two references. I have focused on the most appropriately Lenten use of the symbol, rather than the most obvious or well-known one – hence the omission of Pentecost from the 'fire' symbol's references. The three symbols that make reference to Exodus are in order, and the Exodus story makes good Lenten reading, as it prefigures the story of Jesus' death and resurrection.

A charity calendar

Another calendar idea is that of the charity calendar (see overleaf), like the one I suggested for Advent. I realize not every family, or church leader, will have the time to make calendars with their children, so this one can be used by parents at home or photocopied at church and brought home from Sunday School by the children.

I have taken seven themes, one for each week of Lent. These are broadly based on the Sunday readings for Lent in Year A. The theme of the first week is charity – remembering those who do not have as much as we do. The second is temptation, marking Jesus' temptation in the wilderness. The third week follows the theme of transformation, as the reading is of Jesus' transfiguration on the mountain-top. In the fourth week, we look at the theme of forgiveness and reconciliation – Jesus' conversation with the Samaritan woman and his healing of the government official's son show his ministry extending to those his disciples might consider 'other' or the enemy. The fifth week examines the theme of mission and discipleship (in 2014, this week will include the feast of the Annunciation).

The sixth and seventh weeks relate to the stories leading up to the Passion – the raising of Lazarus and the entry into Jerusalem, with their associated themes of new life and kingship. (Note: on the sixth Wednesday, include any children in your family who have died. If you have had any miscarriages that you and your family have grieved, you can include those children as well.)

The final Saturday in the seventh week asks children to read the Easter Sermon of St Euthemius and invites them to reflect on it, perhaps by making a drawing. I have reproduced the text of the sermon on page 122.

A Lenten charity calendar

	Monday	Tuesday	Wednesday	Thursday	Friday	Saturday
Week 1	Theme: Charity		Ash Wednesday. Some Christians fast on Ash Wednesday, to remember how Jesus fasted for 40 days. Count the tins in your cupboard and put 5p in your box for every tin. Pray for people who do not have enough to eat.	Jesus lived in the wilderness for 40 days. Many people in Britain still do not have a safe place to live. Give 10p for every bed in your house.	God created the world and said that it was good. But people still hurt God's world. Give 5p every time you go in a car today and 2p every time you go on a bus or train.	God told human beings to care for his creation, including the animals. But many animals are endangered. Give 10p for every pet you take care of.
Week 2	Theme: Temptation The first of Jesus' temptations was to turn stones into bread. Give 20p for every loaf of bread in your house.	Jesus' second temptation was to throw himself off the temple and prove to everyone that God's angels would catch him. Have you ever been tempted to do something silly just to prove something? If so, give 10p.	The last of Jesus' temptations was to get power by worshipping the wrong things. Many countries today are still led by people who are greedy and selfish with their power. Give 20p and pray that God will help the leaders of the world to do the right things.	Jesus was tempted in the desert. Find a map of the world and give 5p for every desert you can find.	We are often tempted by food, habits, or thoughts that aren't good for us. Give 5p for every container of junk food in your house.	What have you given up for Lent? Give 2p for every day you've managed to resist temptation so far. Give 5p for every day you've given in.
Week 3	Theme: Transformation As you grow up, you are changing and being transformed all the time. Give 2p for every year of your age.	Jesus' friends climbed a mountain with him and saw him changed, his face shining with glory. Give 10p for every mountain you know of (e.g. Mount Everest).	Education can change people's lives, but millions of children are still too poor to go to school. Their families need them to work, or school isn't free. Give 1p for every book in your room and pray that all children will be given a good education.	Fire changes things – it burns some things to ashes, it melts others. Once some changes are made, they cannot be undone. Give 5p for every fireplace or oven in your house.	Doorways are symbols of moving from one place to another and being changed. Give 5p for every door in your house.	Photographs remind us of how we have grown and changed over the year. Give 2p for every framed photograph on display in your house.

There Is a Season (London: SPCK). Copyright © Margaret Pritchard Houston 2013.

Week 4	**Theme: Forgiveness and reconciliation** Is there somebody you need to say sorry to? Give 10p if you call them or text them to say sorry. Give 5p if you say sorry in person.	Think of all the ways in which people in your family are different from each other. Give 1p for every way you can think of. Now give 5p more to show your love for each other.	There are about 95,000 people in prison in England, Scotland and Wales. Give 10p for every time you have left your house freely today, and pray for people in prison and for people who have been victims of crime.	Give 5p for every time you give somebody a hug today.	Think of someone who is different from you, and who you may have problems getting along with. Try to think of all the ways in which they're the same as you. Give 1p for every way you can think of.	Is there a friend you're not as close to as you used to be? Give them a call or send them a text to say hello.
Week 5	**Theme: Mission and discipleship** Make a list of everything you are good at, and give 2p for each thing you've listed.	Part of Jesus' ministry was healing people who were ill in their bodies or in their minds. With an adult, go through your house and give 10p for every bottle or box of medicine you find.	Jesus said the body is more than clothes. You are Christ's body in the world, but it's very easy to care more about how our bodies look and how fashionable we are than at what our bodies can do and how healthy they are. Look through your sock drawer and give 2p for every pair of socks. Pray for people who don't have enough clothes, and pray that their bodies will be taken care of.	Jesus told us not to let our light hide under a bushel, but to let our lives shine out in the world. Count the light bulbs in your house and give 2p for each one. Give 5p for every candle.	Jesus spent time with people who were considered useless, embarrassing, or bad. He told them they were closer to God than the popular, powerful people. Today, say hello and offer a kind word to somebody who is not popular.	God's spirit gives us all special gifts, and tells us to go out and share our gifts with the world. Think of all the people who share their talents with you, and give 2p for every person you can think of.
Week 6	**Theme: New life** Easter celebrates new life at a time when the world is showing new life. Give 2p for every sign of spring you see today.	Eggs are a symbol of new life and resurrection at Easter. Give 10p for every egg in your refrigerator.	Children are the closest people can come to creating new life, and it was as a child that God chose to come to earth and share his new life with us. Give 5p for every child in your family. Pray for children whose lives are hard.	When we are baptized, we are given new life through water and the Holy Spirit. Give 5p for every tap in your house.	God has promised that when we die, we will have new life that lasts forever in his kingdom. Give 5p for everybody you love who has died. You can include pets.	Jesus' death and new life are shared with us in the bread and wine at church. Give 10p for every meal or snack you eat today.
Week 7	**Theme: Kingship – Holy Week.** Read Mark 11.1–10.	Read Mark 12.1–9.	Read Mark 14.1–11.	Read Mark 14.12–26.	Read John 18.33–37.	Read the Easter Sermon of St Euthemius the Great. Pray, or draw a picture, or go for a walk to help you think about the words.

FROM THE EASTER SERMON OF
ST EUTHEMIUS THE GREAT

Something strange is happening. There is a great silence on earth today. The whole earth is silent, because the King of heaven and earth is dead. God has died, and hell trembles with fear.

Jesus has gone to the place of the dead, to search for Adam and Eve and all who have gone down to darkness and the shadow of death. Jesus approaches them, bearing the cross, the weapon that has won him the victory. He takes them by the hand, and raises them up, and this is what he says:

'Awake, sleepers, and rise from the dead, and Christ will give you light! Rise from the dead, for I am the light of the dead. Out of love for you, I, your God, became a human being and came to earth. For your sake, I died today upon earth. You once reached out to take fruit from a tree, and to save you, I have been nailed to a tree. You were driven out of Paradise, and I have come to lead you to heaven. I did not create you to be held prisoner for ever.

'Rise up! Let us leave this place! For I have died with you and you shall rise with me! The kingdom of heaven has been prepared for you from all eternity!'

There Is a Season (London: SPCK, 2013).

GOOD FRIDAY

Were you there when they crucified my Lord?

INTRODUCTION

The emphasis of this liturgy is on the journey made by Jesus on Good Friday. We walk from station to station, and so make that journey with him. The frequent movement helps keep children from getting restless, as well as allowing them to participate in an interactive way with the story.

The service begins at the font, the symbol of new life. We hear how Jesus was delivered up by Pilate to be crucified, and then begin our journey through four stations of the cross: those at which Jesus meets his mother, Jesus is crucified, Jesus dies, and Jesus is buried in the tomb.

Figure 8 *An Easter garden*

The worship at the stations follows the format 'hymn, reading, reflection, prayers, blowing out a candle'. The reflection takes the form of wondering questions, in which children are invited to pause and reflect on the image provided at each station. The act of blowing out the candle, which concludes each station, reflects the sadness and sorrow of this day – the light of Christ leaving the world before coming back transformed as the new fire at the Easter Vigil. The exception to this pattern is the first station, which does not have a reading, as the station is non-canonical.

The service concludes with a procession to the Easter Garden, when we lay Jesus in the tomb.

The Improperia

Some of the prayers used in this liturgy are from the 'Improperia', a series of reproaches from God to his people which are used in Catholic liturgy on Good Friday and in several Orthodox traditions on Holy Saturday. They follow a standard format. God is shown asking his people, 'My people, what have I done to you? How have I offended you?' He then gives an example from Scripture of how he has shown love towards his people, and they have responded with sin. The imagery of these two actions is often parallel – e.g. 'I scourged your captors and their firstborn sons, but you have brought your scourges down on me.' The people then respond with the line, 'Holy God / Holy and Mighty / Holy Immortal one / have mercy on us.'

Traditionally, the Improperia focused entirely on the ingratitude of God's chosen people, the Jews, and their failure to recognize Jesus as the Messiah. This led, quite rightly, to charges of antisemitism, and the Improperia has been less widely used in recent times.

However, looking at the stories side by side, and finding comparisons between them, is a potent tool in understanding the most holy and profound story in the Bible, that of Christ's death and resurrection. Several years ago, the Revd Grace Pritchard Burson and the Revd Charles Blauvelt wrote new verses to the Improperia and used them in worship at Grace Church in Manchester, New Hampshire, USA. These verses focused on the works of salvation in the New Testament, taking the focus of the piece away from the Jewish people and onto humanity as a whole, including ourselves. I have used some of these verses, with permission, and written some new ones of my own.

SET-UP AND PREPARATION

1 Stations of the cross in the church somewhere. Your church may already have these as a permanent part of its church building. If it doesn't, the children can make them in Sunday School ahead of time, or else you could buy a set of posters. I use laminated posters of paintings made by the nuns at Turvey Abbey, a Catholic Benedictine community in Bedfordshire – they have a depth of imagery and variety of colour which leads to good 'wondering' questions. You can learn more about Turvey Abbey, and the nuns' artwork, from its website (<www.turveyabbey.org.uk/15_artwork.html>).

2 An Easter garden, with a tomb. Ours consisted of a cardboard box painted to look like a tomb (swirls of brown, grey and black, done in five minutes by enthusiastic children), with a circle cut out of it and painted as the stone. It was surrounded by potted flowers, and placed on a green cloth (representing grass). Nearby was a table covered with a hessian cloth; a standing cross and some stones on top of the table represented Golgotha. This was all in a corner of a side chapel in the church. Yours can be as simple or as elaborate as you like, and can be inside or outdoors.

3 A lighted candle, and some way of seating the children, at each station that you use. For a small group, you can have chairs at every station. However, setting up even half a dozen chairs at four different stations is a lot of work! If you don't want to use chairs, or if you have a large group, you can hand out kneelers to the children as they arrive. They can carry their kneelers with them from station to station, and use them as cushions. A third way of providing seating is to spread a blanket or quilt at each station for children to sit on.

4 At the fourth station, you will need flowers in pots, one for each child, and a figure, proportionate in size to your Easter garden, wrapped in 'grave bands' (plain cotton muslin does fine – you could even use a plain white tea towel). We used the detachable figure of Jesus from the 4-in-1 Easter storytelling doll (available from Articles of Faith, among others). If you are absolutely desperate, you can put a Ken doll in a hospital robe and wrap him in a tea towel.

5 If you are not using live musicians, you need a portable CD player (one that can be carried in procession with you, not tied to a wall by a cord) or some other portable form of music, at the fourth station. Alternatively, a helper can be situated next to the church's sound system, finger poised over the 'play' button. The music we used for the procession to the Easter garden was the Bulgarian Orthodox chant of 'The Noble Joseph'. from a CD entitled *Lamentations: Orthodox Chants for Holy Week* by Archangel Voices. It's available for download on Amazon, and is also available from eMusic – the one we used was Track 23. We sang 'Were You There?' and 'O Sacred Head, Sore Wounded' a cappella. You need at least one strong singer to do this well. If you have a children's choir, this is a good opportunity for them to lead the singing.

6 You can include older children and teenagers in this service by using them as readers, or having them lead the wondering questions, or as musicians.

In our Sunday School on Palm Sunday, the children acted out the Passion story and drew their own stations of the cross. Some of these were hung in the church below their corresponding Turvey Abbey station. This gave us an opportunity to compare two different interpretations of the same scene in our wondering questions – for example, the child had included Mary and John at the foot of the cross, while the Turvey Abbey station left them out. I haven't included these wondering questions in the text below, to keep it simple, but this is a good way to include the children even more in the service if you have the time to prepare for it.

As with Ash Wednesday, I have given within the text of the liturgy the wondering questions we used – feel free to change or adapt them for your own congregation.

GOOD FRIDAY LITURGY

Were you there when they crucified my Lord?

We gather in the chairs by the font.

Hymn

> Were you there when they crucified my Lord?
> Were you there when they crucified my Lord?
> Oh, sometimes it causes me to tremble, tremble, tremble.
> Were you there when they crucified my Lord?
>
> Were you there when they nailed him to the tree?
> Were you there when they nailed him to the tree?
> Oh, sometimes it causes me to tremble, tremble, tremble.
> Were you there when they nailed him to the tree?

Reading

Mark 15.15b–20, 22, 24a, 29–32

Reader   A reading from the Gospel according to Mark.

So Pilate whipped Jesus, and delivered him to be crucified. And the soldiers led him away. And they clothed him in a purple cloak, and put a crown of thorns on him. And they began to salute him, saying, 'Hail, King of the Jews!'

And they struck his head with a reed, and spat upon him, and they knelt down in homage to him. And when they had mocked him, they stripped him of the purple cloak, and put his own clothes on him. And they led him out to crucify him.

And they brought him to the place called Golgotha (which means the place of a skull). And they crucified him.

And those who passed by made fun of him, and teased him, saying, 'He saved others; he cannot save himself! Let the Christ, the King of the Jews, come down now from the cross, that we may see and believe.'

THE FIRST STATION: JESUS MEETS HIS MOTHER

We process to the first station, singing:

> O sacred head, sore wounded,
> defiled and put to scorn;
> O kingly head surrounded
> with mocking crown of thorn:

What sorrow mars thy grandeur?
Can death thy bloom deflower?
O countenance whose splendour
the hosts of heaven adore!

We look at the picture and wonder about it.

Leader   I wonder what you can see in this picture.
I wonder how Jesus is feeling.
I wonder what colours you can see.
I wonder where you are in this picture.

Prayer

Leader   My people, what have I done to you?
How have I offended you?
I led you out of Egypt, from slavery to freedom, but you led your Saviour to the cross.

All   **Holy God, Holy and Mighty,**
Holy Immortal One,
have mercy upon us.

A child is invited to blow out the first candle.

We go to the second station, singing:

Thy beauty, long-desirèd,
hath vanished from our sight;
thy power is all expirèd,
and quenched the light of light.
Ah me! for whom thou diest,
hide not so far thy grace:
show me, O Love most highest,
the brightness of thy face.

In thy most bitter passion
my heart to share doth cry,
with thee for my salvation
upon the cross to die.
Ah, keep my heart thus movèd
to stand thy cross beneath,
to mourn thee, well-belovèd,
yet thank thee for thy death.

THE SECOND STATION: JESUS IS NAILED TO THE CROSS

Reading

'Dirge Without Music' by Edna St Vincent Millay

Reader   I am not resigned to the shutting away of loving hearts in the hard ground.
So it is, and so it will be, for so it has been, time out of mind:
Into the darkness they go, the wise and the lovely. Crowned
With lilies and with laurel they go; but I am not resigned.
Lovers and thinkers, into the earth with you.
Be one with the dull, the indiscriminate dust.
A fragment of what you felt, of what you knew,
A formula, a phrase remains – but the best is lost.
The answers quick and keen, the honest look, the laughter, the love,
They are gone. They have gone to feed the roses. Elegant and curled
Is the blossom. Fragrant is the blossom. I know. But I do not approve.
More precious was the light in your eyes than all the roses in the world.
Down, down, down into the darkness of the grave
Gently they go, the beautiful, the tender, the kind;
Quietly they go, the intelligent, the witty, the brave.
I know. But I do not approve. And I am not resigned.

We look at the picture and wonder about it.

Leader   I wonder what you can see in this picture.
I wonder how this picture makes you feel.
I wonder how this picture is different from the last one.
I wonder what Mary and John are feeling.

Prayer

Leader   My people, what have I done to you?
How have I offended you?
I placed you in an abundant garden,
And you have laid hold of me in the garden of Gethsemane.
I became flesh as part of my earthly creation,
and you have nailed that flesh to the cross.

All   **Holy God, holy and mighty,**
Holy Immortal One,
have mercy upon us.

A child blows out the second candle.

We go to the third station, singing:

> My days are few, O fail not,
> with thine immortal power,

to hold me that I quail not
in death's most fearful hour;
that I may fight befriended,
and see in my last strife
to me thine arms extended
upon the cross of life.

THE THIRD STATION: JESUS DIES

Reading

Mark 15.33–34, 37

Reader   And when the sixth hour had come, there was darkness over the whole land until the ninth hour. And at the ninth hour Jesus cried with a loud voice, 'My God, my God, why have you forsaken me?'

And he uttered a loud cry, and breathed his last.

We look at the picture and wonder about it.

Leader   I wonder what you can see in this picture.
I wonder what you like about it? How does it make you feel?
I wonder why Jesus had to die.
I wonder how Jesus' friends felt when he died.
I wonder why the artist used these colours.

We are silent for a minute.

Prayer

Leader   My God, my God, why have you forsaken me? And are so far from my cry and from the words of my distress?
All   **O my God, I cry in the daytime, but you do not answer;**
by night as well, but I find no rest.

Leader   All who see me laugh me to scorn; they curl their lips and wag their heads, saying,
All   **'He trusted in the Lord; let him deliver him;**
let him rescue him, if he delights in him.'

Leader   Yet you are he who took me out of the womb,
and kept me safe upon my mother's breast.
All   **Be not far from me, for trouble is near,**
and there is none to help.

A child blows out the third candle.

We process to the fourth station, singing:

> Were you there when they laid him in the tomb?
> Were you there when they laid him in the tomb?
> Oh, sometimes it causes me to tremble, tremble, tremble.
> Were you there when they laid him in the tomb?

THE FOURTH STATION: JESUS IS LAID IN THE TOMB

Reading

Mark 15.40a, 42–43, 45b–47

Reader   There were also women looking on from afar, among whom were Mary Magdalene, and Mary the mother of Jesus. And when evening had come, Joseph of Arimathea, a respected member of the council, who was also himself looking for the kingdom of God, took courage and went to Pilate, and asked for the body of Jesus. And Pilate granted the body to Joseph. And he bought a linen shroud, and taking him down, wrapped him in the linen shroud, and laid him in a tomb which had been hewn out of the rock; and he rolled a stone against the door of the tomb. Mary Magdalene and Mary the mother of Jesus saw where he was laid.

A child blows out the fourth candle.

Each of the children is given a plant in a pot. One child is given the Jesus figure, wrapped in gravebands. We process to the Easter garden as music plays. We place our plants around the tomb, and a child places Jesus in the tomb and then rolls the stone across the door of the tomb.

When the music is finished, we close with the following prayer:

Leader   My people, what have I done to you?
How have I offended you?
To lead you from slavery to freedom,
I parted the waters of the Red Sea,
But you have taken me captive
And parted my side with a spear.
All   **Holy God, Holy and Mighty,**
Holy Immortal One,
have mercy upon us.

Leader   I was born out of the darkness of my mother's womb
To be the light of the world
And you have extinguished that light
And placed me in the darkness of the grave.
All   **Holy God, Holy and Mighty,**
Holy Immortal One,
have mercy upon us.

The children can remain in the Easter garden, exploring it – smelling the plants, playing with the Jesus doll and the tomb. When they are finished, they and their parents leave the church in silence.

ADDING A EUCHARIST

This being Good Friday, a Eucharist is not appropriate unless it's from the Reserved Sacrament. But in any case, the format of this service as a Stations of the Cross does not easily lend itself to a natural break for communion. I would recommend, therefore, that unless you feel *very* strongly that you should have a Eucharist, you refrain from having one. Children who are used to receiving communion may wonder why there wasn't communion at this service, which could open an interesting discussion.

ADAPTATIONS FOR SCHOOLS

The main challenge with this liturgy, in a school environment, is the movement, and the requirement for an Easter garden in the space used for the liturgy. Without the movement, the hymns become place-fillers rather than guides from one place to the next, and the final gathering around the Easter garden becomes either a crush (if you bring the children out to it) or a spectator sport (if you have one in the hall and bring a select few children up to it to place the flowers and lay Jesus in the tomb). Because of this, I would suggest that if at all possible the original structure of the service be maintained. There are a few ways to do this.

- First, change the scale of the space by turning the playground into the setting for the service. In preparation for the service, one class could make the Easter garden and another the Stations of the Cross on poster-sized paper. Throughout Lent, you could practise the songs in assembly or in music classes. With a small school, the whole school could do the liturgy at once. In larger schools, you may have to divide it between Key Stage 1 and Key Stage 2, but you could probably do the liturgy with up to 100 children at a time, as long as they knew the music and you had enough adult help.

  In this scenario, the stations would have to be placed far enough from each other that the processions have time to form properly – you could have stations 1 and 3 and the Easter garden on one side of the playground and stations 2 and 4 on the other, so you basically zig-zag from one side of the playground to the other as you go through the liturgy.

- Second, if there are two or more halls in your school, split up the liturgy so that it is done in different places. The processions will then take place in corridors, as you move from one hall to the next. You can do stations 1 and 2 in the first hall, without physically moving between them, then stations 3 and 4 in the second hall, and then process outside to finish at the Easter garden.

  Again, it is crucial that the children know the music in advance. With a group this large, participation in the transitional times is essential; otherwise, you just have a crowded, shuffling, distracted group of children in a corridor, and a few adults valiantly singing a hymn.

Depending on the distance between each station, you can re-allocate verses of 'O Sacred Head, Sore Wounded' as needed, to fill the time.

If you absolutely *have* to do this liturgy as a static liturgy held in a single space, without movement, here's how you might approach it:

- Have pictures of the four stations on a screen at the front of the hall, and change them as you go from one to the next.

- The Easter garden should also be at the front of the hall, and children can be chosen to come up and place flowers in it, and lay Jesus in the tomb. In this case, you may wish to do only one verse of 'O Sacred Head, Sore Wounded' at any given time.

EXTENSION ACTIVITIES

As with other seasons, the extension activities related to this liturgy can be carried out in Sunday School in the weeks leading up to and following the liturgy, or as part of a celebration on the day of the liturgy itself.

Since the traditional adult Good Friday service is three hours long, this liturgy provides an opportunity to create a three-hour children's programme on Good Friday, with some activities held before the liturgy and some afterwards. If you do choose to do it this way, however, I would strongly suggest that the children's programme and the adults' three-hour service be led and tidied up by different people! Otherwise, your leaders will have a *very* long day.

Here is a sample schedule for a three-hour programme, assuming the children's service is at 11 a.m. The session runs from 9 a.m. to 12 midday, allowing the children to be out of the church by the time the main service begins at noon.

9.00: Arrival and free choice of activity

9.45: Story

10.00: Singing (practising the hymns from the liturgy)

10.15: Second activity session

10.45: Clean-up and silent procession into the church for the liturgy

11.00: Liturgy

11.30: Third activity session. If you have a noon service, this should be held somewhere away from the path people will be using to enter the church. This will enable children to make a bit of a mess without disrupting the contemplative pre-service atmosphere

Which activities you choose will depend largely on the age, temperament and level of biblical literacy of your children. However, the first two sessions should focus on preparation for the liturgy – making things that will be used during the service, exploring the Good Friday story so the children are familiar with it, and exploring the symbolism of the season, e.g. death and rebirth, trees, stones, light and darkness. In contrast, the processing activities that follow the liturgy give children space to react to the liturgy, to contemplate, and to explore the symbols and imagery used in the liturgy itself. Older children may be able to participate in an activity that applies the issue of social injustice present in the crucifixion story to the modern world, e.g. writing letters for Amnesty International.

Here are some suggestions for the first and second activity sessions. I would not suggest you try to do *all* of these, unless you have lots of volunteers and lots of children – rather, select two or three that you think will work best with your group.

Preparation activities

Here are some suggestions for the first and second activity sessions:

	New to the story	Familiar with the story
Kinaesthetic	**Headstone-rubbing.** If your church has a graveyard, send children out to it with paper and thick crayons, to make rubbings of the headstones. Tell them to	**Bread-baking.** Active children will enjoy the physical activity of mixing bread dough, symbolizing the body of Christ. Use the bread sculpture recipe

find pictures as well as words. This will be a good introduction to Christian symbolism of death and resurrection for children who are not familiar with it.

on page 137, or make unleavened bread which can immediately be turned into shapes using cookie cutters (have a selection of seasonally appropriate ones on hand, e.g. sheep, heart, cross, angel). If your church is open to the idea, use the bread for the Eucharist on Easter morning.

Creative

Painting flowerpots. Terracotta flowerpots take acrylic paint very well. Children can paint their own flowerpot, choose which flower will go in it, and place it in the Easter garden, to be used in the liturgy.

Banner-making. Children can make a banner showing part of the Passion story, to be carried in procession during today's liturgy. The making of banners is described in the All Saints/ All Souls chapter.

Verbal

Story prompts. Have a table with postcard-sized pictures showing different scenes from the Passion. Children can choose one and write a story about what they think is happening. Do not 'correct' the children's stories to make them biblically accurate – this is about using the imagery of the Passion to stimulate their imaginations, not about teaching them. They will learn the biblical story during the next part of the event.

Letter-writing. Children can write letters for Amnesty International on behalf of political prisoners around the world, applying the story of Jesus' unjust arrest and trial to the world we live in today, and living out Christ's message of freedom. **Note:** this would also work as a processing activity.

Suggestions for story time

What you do with the 15-minute story time will also vary, based on the children's age and biblical literacy. If your group is unfamiliar with the story of Christ's death and resurrection, use this time to tell the story of Maundy Thursday and Good Friday. If you want, you can cut singing practice and take the full half hour to tell the story in a dramatic and interactive way – some suggestions for this can be found in the 'Palm Saturday' session of Gretchen Wolff Pritchard's book *Risen With Christ.*[1] The children can play the part of the disciples, having their feet washed, being fed bread and grape juice, and then enter a dark part of the church to experience 'going into the tomb' with Jesus, before being led again into the light. You can use puppets or a DVD, or, if you've spent the time preparing it, the children themselves could present the story. You can have a miniature Godly Play session and do the storytelling that way, or you can read the story from a children's Bible.

If your children are well acquainted with the story, now would be a good time to broaden their imagination through the use of folktale, myth, allegory or modern fiction, through a story related to the Passion. Here are some suggestions:

- *The Tale of Three Trees.*[2] This folktale tells the story of three trees that stood on a hillside. The first tree dreamed of becoming a treasure chest, the second of becoming a ship for a king, and the third of staying on the hilltop and pointing to heaven. All three trees are chopped down, and the first is made into a feed trough for animals, the second into a fishing boat, and the third thrown into a timber yard. It seems their dreams are over. But one night, a young mother places her newborn baby in the feed trough made out of the first tree, and he knows he is holding the greatest treasure in the world. The second tree is out on a lake one night when a storm comes up, and a young man he is carrying calms the storm – and he knows he is carrying the greatest king in the world. The third tree becomes a crucifix for a criminal, but when Easter morning dawns, he knows that whenever people look at him, they will look towards heaven. It is a beautiful story, and children will love seeing how the trees' dreams come true after all, in unexpected ways. There is also a subtle message about the humility of Jesus' kingship.

- *Chicken Sunday.*[3] This autobiographical book by Patricia Polacco introduces children to Easter traditions from different cultures, as well as carrying a message of forgiveness and interfaith understanding. Patricia and her friends are saving up money to buy her friend's grandmother, Miss Eula Mae, an Easter hat. They are outside the hat shop one day when some older boys throw eggs at the shop and run away. The owner (who is a Russian Jew) thinks Patricia and her friends did it. To prove their innocence, they spend hours decorating Easter eggs in the traditional Russian style of *pysanky* and bring them to the hat shop owner. He is so moved by their offering that he allows them to sell the eggs from his shop. Finally, he makes them a gift of the hat they wanted. The portrayal of the Easter service in the African-American church is joyous and uplifting, and the final image of a grown-up Patricia and her friends tending Miss Eula Mae's grave can serve as a launching point for a discussion about death, resurrection and Easter.

- *Nana Upstairs and Nana Downstairs.*[4] This book by Tomie de Paola is a moving exploration of the death of a beloved grandmother. If children in your group are struggling with bereavement in their own lives, Good Friday is an excellent time to bring up questions about their loss and how their Christian faith may be a source of hope and joy.

Processing activities

Here are some ideas for third session activities:

	New to the story	Familiar with the story
Kinaesthetic	**Walking a labyrinth.** A labyrinth allows children a calm, contemplative experience through which to process their thoughts. If you are lucky enough to have one in your church or church garden, wonderful. If not, SensoryEdge (<www.sensoryedge.com>) sells a classroom rug with a labyrinth on it – but you may have to order it from abroad. However, it could be a great investment, used for years to come. Alternatively, <yourdecoshop.co.uk> sells a labyrinth transfer that could be placed on linoleum, laminate or tiled floors.	**A sense table.** Have a table set out with objects relating to the story which engage all five senses. For example: *Smell*: myrrh, olive oil *Taste*: matzoh, bitter herbs, apple sauce, grape juice (some of the things Christ and the disciples would have eaten/drunk at the Last Supper, a Passover seder) *Touch*: nails, wood, stones *Sight*: portrayals of the crucifixion in different artistic styles *Hearing*: a selection of CDs with Lent/Easter music, e.g. Orthodox chant, Anglican hymns

135

Figure 9 *A Holy Week sense table*

Creative   **Book-making.** Provide pieces of paper with the different parts of the story on them; use the Godly Play script[5] or write your own adaptation, or use the original language of one of the Gospels, depending on the children's ages. The children can illustrate whichever scene they choose. When they're finished, make covers with two pieces of card and bind into a book (either use a binding machine or punch holes through the sheets and seal with brads).

'Decorating the Alleluia'. If you have hidden an Alleluia (see Ash Wednesday), now would be a good time to take it out and decorate it, hiding it again so it can be found, transformed, on Easter morning.

Verbal   **Magnetic poetry.** Individual magnetic boards and a selection of magnetic poetry sets can give children a structured way to express their feelings (it's less intimidating than a blank page). You can take photos of their creations to preserve them. This activity is equally accessible to those with high and those with low biblical literacy.

Bread sculpture: challah bread

This simple, delicious bread is a staple from my childhood, and is one of many recipes for the traditional Jewish Sabbath bread called challah. What makes this recipe particularly suitable for use with children is the way the bread dough can be sculpted, to make wonderful baked artworks.

It's also virtually foolproof – even if the water is too hot and the yeast doesn't prove as well as it should, and it doesn't really rise, as has happened at several of our church's events, it still tastes good! (Note: rising can be helped along by placing the dough, with a damp cloth across the top of the bowl, in the bathroom with a hot tap or shower running!)

Ideas for Good Friday/Easter bread sculptures include:

- an empty tomb

- a lamb

- a cross with flowers on the front of it

- a communion cup

- a decorated heart

- an angel

- a wheat sheaf (the wheat dies and rises, to feed us)

- Jonah and the whale (after being swallowed by the whale for three days, Jonah was 'resurrected' and given new life, in a prefiguring of Christ's resurrection).

CHALLAH BREAD SCULPTURES

500 ml warm water

1 packet yeast

60 ml oil

60 ml honey (use the same measuring cup, straight after the oil – the honey will slide right out of it!)

2 teaspoons salt

Flour (as much as is needed to turn it to dough – approximately 800 g – and more for kneading and shaping)

1 Pour the water into a large bowl and add the yeast. Let it prove for about five minutes, then add the oil, honey and salt. Mix.

2 Add the flour, about 100 g at a time, stirring each time. When the mixture has come together in a sticky dough, turn it out onto a well-floured surface and knead, adding more flour as you go if necessary. Place the kneaded dough back in the bowl. (To involve children, you can divide the dough up and give them each a bit to knead.)

3 Set to rise in a warm space, with a damp tea towel across the top of the bowl, for about an hour, until the dough has approximately doubled in size.

4 Punch the risen dough down, and cover a workplace with flour. Sprinkle a little extra flour on top of the dough.

5 The dough can then be shaped – encourage children to think of an appropriate shape for the occasion. As you shape the dough, you may need to add small amounts of flour to keep it from sticking to the children's hands. Supervise children so the flour is not dumped in huge handfuls over the dough. The basic shapes that you will use to sculpt are balls, snakes and large oblongs. The sculptures are flat, not freestanding, and should be made on the surface they will be baked on (if using a baking sheet, it should be greased). Balls can be made by rolling a small amount of bread in your palms. Snakes can be made by holding the bread between your palms and making quick back and forth movements, as you would with modelling clay. Oblongs can be shaped on the surface itself. Scoring can be done using a small knife.

6 When you've shaped the dough, set it to rise again, then brush it with egg or oil, and bake. Smaller sculptures can bake in about 20 minutes at 190° C/gas mark 5, while larger ones may take up to 45 minutes.

Some examples of how you can shape the dough are shown in Figure 10 (these are my own work, not children's work). The angel's body is one large oblong, the wings are triangles and the rest is all balls and snakes. The tops of the ears of wheat are three small snakes, plaited, while the stalks are snakes and the binding is made up of two snakes twisted together.

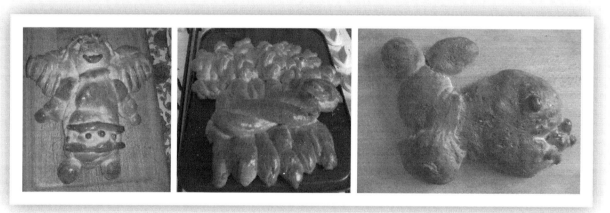

Figure 10 *Challah bread sculptures: an angel, a wheatsheaf, and Jonah and the whale*

EXTENSIONS FOR HOME

There are many ways in which parents can support children in their walk through Holy Week. The Lenten calendar available in the Ash Wednesday chapter continues through this time, but there are other ways of making Holy Week special for children.

Good Friday, in particular, should be observed in the home by making it a day of quiet and solemnity. Institute a ban on television, the internet, the PlayStation, and any music that is not solemn (it doesn't have to be sacred, but today is not a day for *ABBA Gold*). Food should be simple – no sweets, crisps or fizzy drinks. Spend the day in contemplative activities. If you have active, physically demanding children, engage them in one of the nature-related activities in the Easter chapter – these are also appropriate for Holy Week and Triduum.

Artistic activities

If your child is artistically inclined, I suggest the following:

- The Ukrainian tradition of *pysanky* Easter egg dyeing is a wonderful way for older children to prepare for Easter. This technique is based on the principle of wax relief – a pysanky kit has six coloured dyes, and the artist begins by putting wax on each part of the egg that is to remain white. The egg is then dipped in the yellow dye, and when it is removed, the artist covers each part of the egg that will remain yellow with wax. This technique is continued with all six dyes, and, at the end, all the wax is melted off. It is a delicate, precise technique, and one egg usually takes approximately three hours to complete. Between the ages of 10 and 22, however, I would routinely spend several hours each day during Holy Week completely absorbed in my *pysanky* (and I got pretty good at it, if I may say so!). It was a meditative experience, and my imagery grew more sophisticated as my understanding of Easter grew – and the egg itself is a potent symbol of new life. *Pysanky* kits are available in the UK from the Association of Ukrainians in Great Britain (<www.augb.co.uk/ukrainian-easter-eggs-pysanky.php>) and come with all the materials you will need, as well as a leaflet explaining traditional *pysanky* imagery and its meanings, much of which is explicitly Christian (e.g. three-sided designs symbolizing the Trinity).

- The technique of wax resist can be adapted for younger children by providing them with coloured crayons. They can use these to draw on a plain hard-boiled duck egg and can then dye the egg in a mixture of ordinary food dye and white vinegar (use a *lot* of vinegar relative to dye). Encourage children to decorate their egg with symbols of the Passion and Resurrection, e.g. cross, heart, butterfly, sun, flower, communion cup.

- Many of the art projects recommended for churches will also work at home, particularly painting flowerpots and illustrating a book showing the story of the Passion.

- Make your own tabletop Easter garden on a baking sheet. Line the sheet with moss, cut a door out of a small cardboard box painted to be a tomb. Make a cross out of twigs and string, and fill in the garden with trees from Playmobil or model railway sets. To represent Jesus, wrap a doll's house doll ('hospital' ones work well, as they're in robes) in fabric and place him in the tomb. On Easter Eve, after the children have gone to bed, parents can unwrap 'Jesus' and place him outside the tomb, leaving the wrappings inside it.

- Visit a gallery or museum with your child and discuss the Christian imagery used in the artwork. If you like, you can bring along a sketch pad and some drawing materials, choose an inspiring room, and sit and draw with your child. Encourage your child to choose a religious subject, using some of the imagery you've seen. The peaceful atmosphere of a gallery, and the meditative activity of becoming immersed in drawing, are very appropriate for Good Friday.

Cooking activities

Food is an integral part of our celebrations together, but it takes on a particularly sacred meaning during Holy Week and Easter, when we meditate on Christ's body, given for us, and remembered in the bread and wine of the Eucharist.

The use of lamb as a traditional Easter food recalls the image of Jesus as the sacrificial lamb of God, the *Agnus Dei*. This tradition has its origins in the Jewish Passover feast, when lamb is eaten to recall the sacrificial lambs whose blood saved the Israelites from the Angel of Death before the Exodus. Lamb is traditionally eaten as part of a Passover seder, which is what the Last Supper was – this image has therefore become associated with the death of Jesus, whose blood saved all humanity from death and sin.

Another traditional Good Friday/Easter food, hot cross buns, symbolize the crucifixion (and, according to food writer Elizabeth David, were originally made from leftovers from the dough used for communion bread).

Here are some recipes that can be made with children. Of course children should be properly supervised when near heat and sharp objects!

HOT CROSS BUNS

Makes approx. 20

These are by far the best hot cross buns I've ever tasted. They are much denser and richer than the fluffy shop-bought kind, and the glaze is nice and lemony.

Children will enjoy helping you mix the ingredients, knead the dough, shape the buns, and particularly apply the glaze! As with all bread-baking activities, this one has eucharistic overtones that you can comment on with your children as you work. Note that this recipe involves storing the dough overnight in the refrigerator, so do the first part on Maundy Thursday and finish on Good Friday.

For the buns:

240 ml milk

2 tablespoons yeast

100 g sugar

2 teaspoons salt

150 ml olive oil

1½ teaspoons cinnamon

½ teaspoon nutmeg

4 eggs

650 g flour

175 g currants or raisins

1 egg white

For the glaze:

160 g icing sugar

2 teaspoons finely chopped lemon zest (you can use orange zest if you prefer the flavour)

1–2 teaspoons lemon extract (or orange juice)

1½ tablespoons milk

1 In a small saucepan, heat the milk until it is warm but not hot. Pour the warm milk into a bowl and sprinkle yeast over it. Mix to dissolve and allow to prove for 5 minutes.

2 Stirring constantly, add the sugar, salt, oil, cinnamon, nutmeg and eggs. Gradually mix in the flour; the dough will be wet and sticky. Turn out on a floured surface and knead. When the dough is smooth, cover the bowl and let the dough rise for 30–45 minutes.

3 Knead again, for about 1 minute, then add currants or raisins and knead until well mixed. Place dough in a buttered dish and chill in refrigerator overnight.

4 The next morning, remove the dough. Split it in half, then in half again, and then split each of the four sections into five pieces.

5 Line your baking trays with greaseproof paper and place the buns on the trays. Leave in a warm, draught-free place for approximately 1½ hours, until the buns have nearly doubled in size. While they are rising, heat your oven to 200° C/gas mark 6.

6 After the buns have risen, score the top of each with a sharp knife to make a cross shape, then bake them for 10 minutes at 200° C. Then turn the heat down to 175° C/gas mark 4 and bake for 15 minutes more, or until golden brown.

7 Meanwhile, whisk together the ingredients for the glaze. Apply the glaze with a spoon or brush immediately upon removing the buns from the oven. Serve warm if possible.

UNLEAVENED BREAD

Unleavened bread is traditionally eaten by Jews during Passover. The traditional meaning of this is that the Jews had to leave Egypt in such a hurry there was no time to let the bread rise; however, other meanings are being debated.

This recipe is easy to do with children, because there are no breaks while the dough is left to rise or chill – you can do it all at once! The children can shape their own bread, or use cookie cutters (use Easter shapes – lamb, cross, etc.).

2 eggs	120 g butter
360 ml warm milk	550 g flour
120 ml honey	2 teaspoons salt

1 Beat the eggs, milk, honey and butter together and add the salt.

2 Add the flour gradually. Knead until smooth.

3 Roll the mixture to a thickness of ¼ in (5 mm), then cut into shapes. Place the shaped pieces on a greased baking tray.

4 Bake at 200° C/gas mark 6 for 15–20 minutes until golden brown. During the first few minutes of baking, prick any bubbles that may form with a fork.

EASTER

Alleluia! Christ is risen!

INTRODUCTION

This liturgy is based on the format of the Great Vigil of Easter and its purpose, therefore, is the build-up and release of tension. It consists of four sections:

1 Hearing and remembering God's saving works in history. This takes the form of acting out three of the stories from the Great Vigil – Creation, Exodus and the Dry Bones. All three are, in their own way, foreshadowings of the Resurrection. The Creation brings light out of darkness (as does the Resurrection), the Exodus brings God's people from slavery to freedom (as does the Resurrection, in freeing us from our slavery to sin), and the Dry Bones is a prophecy of the dead rising again (reminding us that it is not only Jesus who is risen from the dead, but, ultimately, all of us, through his resurrection). This last section should be done reverently, and with a sense of hushed anticipation. It is not raucous or silly. As far as possible, it should take place in relative darkness.

2 Lighting the new fire and singing the Exsultet. This marks the beginning of our Easter celebration. We are, symbolically, at the tomb, hearing the good news, but not believing it yet. There should, as much as possible, be a feeling that we are suspended in liturgical mid-air – about to spill over into noisy joy as we proclaim the resurrection.

3 The proclamation of the Resurrection. The final element in the build-up of tension is the sermon of John Chrysostom, which actually serves as a bridge between Lent and Easter – when it begins, we are in Lent, but by the time it finishes, we have proclaimed Christ risen. This finishes with the door to the 'Easter space' being flung open, the Hallelujah chorus playing at full volume, and the congregation shouting 'He is risen indeed!' at the top of their voices. If possible, the sermon should be read with the children gathered closely around the door, still in relative darkness; when we do it that way, it feels as if we are metaphorically in the tomb. Then, when the words 'Christ is risen!' come and we are allowed to pour out of the dark, enclosed space into the big, light room full of flowers and candles and cake, we have metaphorically risen from the dead with Jesus.

4 The celebration. This first part of this consists of sharing celebratory food together – cake that has previously been set out on the table in the Easter space. If you're brave, you can use the altar – the imagery of a celebratory cake that we share as part of our worship is, at its heart, eucharistic. The Eucharist is special, different from ordinary food. So are party cakes. I am not saying that a party cake is the Eucharist, but rather that the symbolism of the two are similar, and sharing a party cake that has sat on the altar, as part of communal worship, can help remind children how special that *other* food on the altar is. The celebration finishes with a blessing and the conclusion of 'Lord of the Dance', the earlier verses of which have been sung in sections throughout the first part of the liturgy. The blessing should be done with the children in a circle around the table – this puts you in perfect position to finish the liturgy with a joyful dance

around the altar, as you sing 'Lord of the Dance'. The children can simply hold hands and circle in one direction for the verses and in the other direction for the chorus. If the children know how to perform the dance movement known as a grapevine, or you take a moment to teach them, even better.

There is a temptation, with anything reverential and full of tension, to diffuse that tension through silliness and clowning. This must be avoided at all costs. There may be giggles, particularly among the older ones – there usually are when you are doing something taut and full of anticipation with children. It's one way they have of releasing tension. There will probably not be silent, reverential awe at all times throughout this service. However, your children's giggles should come from *real emotion*, processed through a vague pre-adolescent self-consciousness, not the kind that come from hamming up the slapstick elements of a festival because the adults are uncomfortable with real liturgics.

SET-UP AND PREPARATION

I've done this liturgy on the first Sunday after Easter, as many of our children are away for Easter and thus have not yet celebrated Easter with their home church family. It is performed as a Sunday School lesson, and therefore takes place in parts of the church building other than the sanctuary.

However, it would be even more effective on Holy Saturday, at night, just after sunset. The imagery of light and darkness would be more vivid, and you would be able to use the sanctuary. Many churches struggle to hold the Easter Vigil early enough in the evening to enable families to attend while late enough to give adults that 'middle of the night' feeling and ensure that it takes place in real darkness, even when Easter is late. To settle this problem, you could hold this service for families at 8.30 p.m. and have the full Easter Vigil at 10.30 or 11.00 at night (or even at 5 o'clock on Easter morning).

The liturgy includes a number of interactive lessons: the Red Sea, the Dry Bones. The reader will need to pause at certain points to instruct the children in where to move and what to do. This should be done as unobtrusively as possible, without a break in the awe-struck mood.

You will need:

1 Readers, and someone to sing the Exsultet. The leader can do all this, if necessary, but it is better to spread it out. The Exsultet *can* be spoken, rather than sung, but if there is any way for it to be sung, it should be.

2 A starting place that can be kept in almost complete darkness. We use a stairwell, as we usually do this liturgy with around a dozen children, but you may need a larger space.

3 A desert area. This can be any space that's relatively plain and open. There needs to be somewhere at the edge of this space that can represent the Red Sea.

4 Blue fabric with which to create the Red Sea. You could hang this over a door and open the door for the children to go through the Red Sea, or two adults could hold pieces of fabric, separating them to allow the children to walk through. Or you could hang the fabric over a line, and the children could push it apart.

5 A Babylon area. Again, this needs to be somewhere relatively open. It might be the chancel of your church or a balcony, an outdoor area or a community space. The only requirement is that there be enough room for the children to spread out and lie down, and there should be a

minimum of distractions – so a playspace would not be a good idea. Either way, it should be fairly close to the outside space where you will be lighting the new fire. We use our porch for both the Babylon space and the lighting of the new fire so there is no need to move from one to the other.

6 An Easter space. We use our Sunday School room. This should be separate from where the rest of the service takes place. Ideally, it should be your sanctuary – the early parts of the service take place in the fringes of your church building, and then you enter its very heart for the proclamation of the Resurrection. The children should not have had to pass through it – or, ideally, have seen it – before this point in the service.

7 In the Easter space, set up a table with white linen, flowers, and a cake with plates and forks. (If you have children with gluten allergies, don't forget to have gluten-free baked goods on the table as well.) You can also do the processing activities in this space, directly after the liturgy, so you'll need to set those up as well.

8 Candles for all the children. Younger children may use flameless candles.

9 A large candle for the leader at the beginning.

10 Castanets, or something else that can make a rattling sound.

11 Something in which to light the new fire. This should be outdoors. A metal bucket filled with dry wood and newspaper is the usual way of doing this, but you could use a disposable barbecue, or build a bonfire in your church garden (better for rural parishes, I think, than urban ones!). Next to the fire you should have a bucket of water and a small branch with leaves. If you're doing this liturgy at night, I strongly recommend you use an actual fire, although you can use a Paschal candle instead.

12 A fire extinguisher powerful enough to subdue your new fire if needed, on hand but discreetly hidden away. Nothing ruins the symbolism of the new fire more than Health and Safety regulations about containing it!

13 A portable CD/mp3 player with the Hallelujah Chorus cued and ready to go.

THE EASTER LITURGY

Alleluia! Christ is risen!

We start in the darkness.

Reading

Genesis 1.1–3, 5b; paraphrased summary of Genesis 1; Genesis 2.2

Reader   A reading from the book of Genesis.

In the beginning, God created the heavens and the earth. The whole earth was in darkness, and the Spirit of God moved over the face of the earth. And God said, 'Let there be light,' and there was light.

(The leader lights a single candle.)

And God saw that the light was good. And there was evening, and there was morning, one day.

God created everything in the world – the sky, the oceans, the sun and moon and stars, plants, animals, fish, birds, and people.

And God saw that it was good.

Thus the heavens and earth were created, and all that was in them. And on the seventh day, God rested from all the work he had done.

We move to the desert area, singing.

Hymn

I danced in the morning, when the world was begun
And I danced in the moon and the stars and the sun.
I came down from heaven and I danced on the earth.
At Bethlehem, I had my birth.

Dance, then, wherever you may be.
I am the Lord of the dance, said he,
And I'll lead you all, wherever you may be,
And I'll lead you all in the dance, said he.

Reader   God chose two people, Abraham and Sarah, to be the mother and father of his Chosen People. Abraham and Sarah had children and grandchildren and great-grandchildren, and they lived in the land of Canaan. But when there was no food in Canaan, they went to Egypt, where they became a people great in number. And Pharaoh became afraid, and made them slaves. But God chose Moses to set the people free. In the middle of the night, the people of Israel left Egypt, and camped on the shore of the Red Sea.

Reading

Exodus 14.10, 13–17, 19–21

Reader   A reading from the book of Exodus.

When Pharaoh drew near, the people of Israel lifted up their eyes, and behold, the Egyptians were marching after them; and they were in great fear. And the people of Israel cried out to the LORD.

And Moses said to the people, 'Fear not, stand firm, and see the salvation of the LORD, which he will work for you today; for the Egyptians whom you see today, you shall never see again. The LORD will fight for you, and you have only to be still.' The LORD said to Moses, 'Why do you cry to me? Tell the people of Israel to go forward. Lift up your rod, and stretch out your hand over the sea and divide it, that the people of Israel may go on dry ground through the sea. And I will harden the hearts of the Egyptians so that they shall go in after them, and I will get glory over Pharaoh and all his host, his chariots, and his horsemen.'

Then the angel of God who went before the host of Israel moved and went behind them; and the pillar of cloud moved from before them and stood behind them, coming between the host of Egypt and the host of Israel.

Then Moses stretched out his hand over the sea; and the LORD drove the sea back by a strong east wind all night, and made the sea dry land, and the waters were divided. And the people of Israel went into the midst of the sea on dry ground, the waters being a wall to them on their right hand and on their left.

Hymn

As we sing the hymn, the children pass through the middle of the blue cloth and take their seats in the Babylon area.

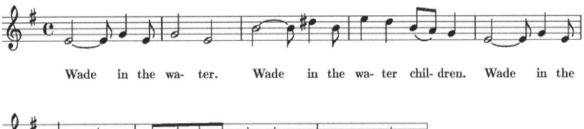

Wade in the water. Wade in the water children. Wade in the water, God's a-gonna trouble the water.

(Repeat until all children are in their places.)

Reader   God led the people of Israel out of slavery, into the land of Promise. But the people did not follow God's laws. They lied and cheated and stole from each other. They fought and hurt and killed each other. And one day their enemies came, and burned the holy city of Jerusalem, and led them as slaves to Babylon.

In Babylon, God chose a man named Ezekiel to be a prophet, to tell the people God's plans for them.

Ezekiel had this dream.

We will act out Ezekiel's dream, which begins in a valley full of bones. So I need all of you to lie down, like bones in the desert.

(All the children lie down.)

Reading

Ezekiel 37

Reader   A reading from the book of the prophet Ezekiel.

The hand of the LORD was upon me, and he brought me out by the Spirit of the LORD, and set me down in the midst of the valley; it was full of bones. And he led me round among them; and behold, there were very many upon the valley; and lo, they were very dry. And he said to me, 'Son of man, can these bones live?' And I answered, 'O Lord GOD, you know.'

Again he said to me, 'Prophesy to these bones, and say to them, O dry bones, hear the word of the Lord. Thus says the Lord GOD to these bones: Behold, I will cause breath to enter you, and you shall live. And I will lay sinews upon you, and will cause flesh to come upon you, and cover you with skin, and put breath in you, and you shall live; and you shall know that I am the LORD.'

(As the following is read, the leader shakes the castanets, and the children stand up, using jerky movements. They then freeze in a standing position.)

So I prophesied as I was commanded; and as I prophesied, there was a noise, and behold, a rattling; and the bones came together, bone to its bone. And as I looked, there were sinews on them, and flesh had come upon them, and skin had covered them; but there was no breath in them.

Then he said to me, 'Prophesy to the breath, prophesy, son of man, and say to the breath, Thus says the Lord GOD: Come from the four winds, O breath, and breathe upon these slain, that they may live.'

(As the following is read, all the children begin to move as though a wind is blowing – freely, loosely – then come to stand in orans position.)

So I prophesied as he commanded me, and the breath came into them, and they lived, and stood upon their feet, an exceedingly great host. Then he said to me, 'Son of man, these bones are the whole house of Israel. Behold, they say, "Our bones are dried up, and our hope is lost; we are clean cut off."'

'Therefore prophesy, and say to them, Thus says the Lord GOD: Behold, I will open your graves, and raise you from your graves, O my people; and I will bring you home into the land of Israel. And you shall know that I am the LORD, when I open your graves, and raise you from your graves, O my people. And I will put my Spirit within you, and you shall live, and I will place you in your own land; then you shall know that I, the LORD, have spoken, and I have done it, says the LORD.'

We move to where the new fire will be lit, singing:

> Dance, then, wherever you may be.
> I am the Lord of the dance, said he,
> And I'll lead you all, wherever you may be,
> And I'll lead you all in the dance, said he.

(Repeat until all are gathered by the new fire.)

The leader lights the new fire.

Leader   Once you were in darkness, but now you are light in the Lord. Walk as children of the light.

The children light individual candles from the new fire or Paschal candle. As the candles are lit, the Exsultet is said or sung:

Singer   Rejoice now, heavenly hosts and choirs of angels,
and let your trumpets shout Salvation
for the victory of our mighty King.
This is the night, when you brought the children of Israel
out of bondage in Egypt and led them through the
Red Sea on dry land.
This is the night, when Christ broke the bonds of death and hell,
and rose victorious from the grave.
How holy is this night, when wickedness is put to flight, and
sin is washed away.
How blessed is this night, when earth and heaven are joined
and man is reconciled to God ...
May Christ, the Morning Star who knows no setting, find this flame
ever burning – he who gives his light to all creation, and who lives
and reigns for ever and ever. Amen.

The leader, who may have help from some of the children, then takes a branch and dips it in the water next to the new fire. The leader sprinkles the congregation with the water, saying:

Leader   You have died with Christ, and, through baptism, share with him in his resurrection. Receive this water and the new life it brings.

We process to the Easter area, singing:

> I danced for the scribes and the Pharisee,
> But they would not dance and they wouldn't follow me.
> I danced for the fishermen – for James and John.
> They came with me and the dance went on.
>
> Dance, then, wherever you may be.
> I am the Lord of the dance, said he.
> And I'll lead you all, wherever you may be,
> And I'll lead you all in the dance, said he.
>
> I danced on the Sabbath and I cured the lame.
> The holy people said it was a shame.

> They whipped and they stripped and they hung me high,
> And they left me there on a cross to die.
>
> Dance, then, wherever you may be.
> I am the Lord of the dance, said he.
> And I'll lead you all, wherever you may be,
> And I'll lead you all in the dance, said he.

We gather outside the door to the Easter area.

Reading

From the Easter Sermon of St John Chrysostom

Reader   Whoever is devout and a lover of God, come, enjoy this beautiful and radiant Feast of Feasts!
Whoever is a good and faithful servant, rejoice, and enter into the joy of your Lord.
Enter all of you, into the joy of our Lord, and whether first or last receive your reward.
O rich and poor, one with another dance for joy! The table is rich-laden, feast royally,
all of you! The calf is fatted; let no one go forth hungry!

Let all partake of the Feast of Faith. Let all receive the riches of goodness.
Let none mourn their sins, for Pardon has dawned from the Tomb!
Let no one fear Death, for the Saviour's death has set us free!

He that was taken by Death has annihilated it! He descended into Hell, and took
Hell captive! Hell was embittered when it tasted his flesh.

It was embittered, for it was abolished!
It was embittered, for it was mocked!
It was embittered, for it was purged!
It was embittered, for it was despoiled!
It was embittered, for it was *bound in chains*!

It laid hold of a mortal body, and found that it had seized God!
It laid hold of earth, but confronted heaven!
It seized what it saw, but crumbled before what it had not seen!
O Death, where is thy sting? O Hell, where is thy victory?

Christ is risen, and Hell is overthrown!
Christ is risen, and the demons are fallen!
Christ is risen, and the angels rejoice!
Christ is risen, and life reigns!
Christ is risen, and *not one dead remains in the tombs*!
For Christ being raised from the dead has become the first-fruits of them that slept.
To him be glory and dominion through all the ages of ages!

Leader   Christ is risen!
All   **He is risen indeed!**

Leader   Christ is risen!!!
All   **He is risen indeed!!!**

Leader   CHRIST IS RISEN!!!!!
All   **HE IS RISEN INDEED!!!!!**

The Hallelujah Chorus plays. The door to the Easter area is flung open, and we are invited to come in and share in the celebration.

When everyone has finished their cake, the leader gathers everyone in a circle round the table for the blessing.

Leader   Alleluia! Christ is risen!

All   **He is risen indeed! Alleluia!**

Leader   Christ, who is risen, lives for ever. Let us pray together, in the name of the living Lord.

(During the prayer, the leader goes to every child present and, with his or her thumb, makes the sign of the cross on each child's forehead.)

Leader   Lord, make us instruments of your peace.
Where there is hatred, let us sow love.
Where there is injury, pardon.
Where there is doubt, faith.
Where there is despair, hope.
Where there is darkness, light.
Grant that we may not so much seek to be consoled as to console,
to be understood as to understand,
to be loved as to love.
For it is in giving that we receive.
It is in pardoning that we are pardoned.
And it is in dying that we are born to eternal life. Amen!

All   **Amen!**

Hymn

I danced on a Friday when the sky turned black.
It's hard to dance with the devil on your back.
They buried my body and they thought I'd gone.
But I am the dance and I still go on!

Dance, then, wherever you may be.
I am the Lord of the dance, said he.
And I'll lead you all, wherever you may be,
And I'll lead you all in the dance, said he.

They cut me down, and I leapt up high!
I am the life that will never, never die!
I'll live in you if you'll live in me.
I am the Lord of the dance, said he.

Dance, then, wherever you may be.
I am the Lord of the dance, said he.
And I'll lead you all, wherever you may be,
And I'll lead you all in the dance, said he.

Dance, then, wherever you may be.
I am the Lord of the dance, said he.
And I'll lead you all, wherever you may be,
And I'll lead you all in the dance, said he.

Leader   Alleluia! Alleluia! Go in the joy of the risen Christ, who lives for ever!
All   **Amen! Alleluia!**

ADDING A EUCHARIST

This liturgy easily lends itself to the inclusion of a Eucharist. The Easter area of the liturgy can be the chancel, decorated in advance with Easter flowers, and the altar laid with the elements. When the transition is made from Lent to Easter, with the proclamation of the Resurrection and the playing of the Hallelujah Chorus, the Children stream into the chancel area and surround the altar. The service then leads directly into a Eucharist and the blessing, before finishing with the final verses of 'Lord of the Dance'.

The provision of a 'party with cake' in the middle of the service is an ersatz Eucharist anyway.

ADAPTATIONS FOR SCHOOLS

This liturgy, like the one for Good Friday, includes quite a lot of movement. However, it is possible to do it with a whole school, or with several classes at once, if time and thought are put into the preparations.

Here are some suggestions for making it successful and as stress-free as possible:

• Hold the first part of the liturgy – the three lessons, the lighting of the new fire, and the Exsultet – in one place. If at all possible you should do this part outside, as you'll be lighting the new fire. If you're doing it indoors, use a large candle instead, though it's not as effective. The school should then process together to the second location, which is set up for the party (you could use the school hall or a church building). Instead of trying to sing the verses of 'Lord of the Dance' that are reproduced here, you can use the following, which is like a chant and easy for a large group, moving together, to sing together (it's available for download from Amazon, so you can have a portable music player playing it to help you keep in time):

> He is Lord. He is Lord.
> He is risen from the dead and he is Lord.
> Every knee shall bow, every tongue confess
> That Jesus Christ is Lord.

• Individual classes could each present one of the lessons as a performance, instead of having the whole school act them out. One class would do Creation, one Exodus and one the Dry Bones. Stick to the printed text as closely as possible.

• Instead of doing art activities along with having cake after the proclamation of the Resurrection, finish the liturgy with cake and the Prayer of St Francis. Since 'Lord of the Dance' has not yet appeared in this liturgy, the whole school could sing it in its entirety here (see pages 157–8), before you send children back to their classrooms for the activities.

EXTENSION ACTIVITIES

Preparation activities

This liturgy requires very little preparation if the children have already experienced Palm Sunday and/or Good Friday. Holy Week provides its own preparation for the Great Vigil of Easter, and if your children have been involved in Holy Week at all, you can feel confident going into this liturgy without further preparation.

- Otherwise, you may want to begin by telling or acting out the story of the Passion, or showing a film of it. Many film versions of the Passion are unsuitable for children either for reasons of gratuitous violence, tackiness or bad theology. However, here are a few that could work:

  - *Jesus Christ Superstar*, from the Last Supper onwards (probably better for older children);

  - *Godspell*, from 'On the Willows' onwards (may require some explanation about what is happening);

  - *The Mysteries* by South African theatre company Yimimangaliso. This is, quite simply, the best theatrical version of biblical stories I have ever seen. Each actor speaks in his or her native language, so only about one-quarter of the dialogue is in English – because of this, the actions, emotions, and theatrical set-pieces are phenomenally clear and well done. The crucifixion is moving and tragic without being lurid, and the resurrection is immensely powerful. Produced by Heritage Theatre, the availability of this DVD in the UK fluctuates – however, it is fairly consistently available from Amazon USA, which is fine if you have a multi-region DVD player.

- Children can make a mural depicting the different scenes of the story, or illustrate pages that you can later turn into a book.

- If you have a bit more time and energy, you can begin by sharing a simple meal together. Ensure that bread and grape juice are included. Near the end of the meal, one person stands and begins telling or reading the story of the Last Supper, acting it out by using bread and grape juice from the table. Children can then take turns washing each other's feet. Another person then tells the story of Jesus' arrest and trials, and as a third person tells of the crucifixion, everyone processes together into the darkened church, waiting in silence for the liturgy to begin. (Note: don't make children wait more than a few minutes in silence – this will be more than enough to create the atmosphere. Adults can meditate in darkness for half an hour before the Vigil, but children cannot.)

- If sitting in darkness is too difficult for your children, you can bridge the gap by using the litany of the saints from the All Saints/All Souls chapter and processing around the church in semi-darkness,
  then extinguishing all the lights immediately before the service begins.

Processing activities

These can be done either as part of the liturgy itself (during the break where cake is shared), or directly afterwards. They can also be done in a separate session later on in the Easter season.

- Banners and bread-baking are appropriate for any time of year. By making banners several times during the year, you create a library of banners ready to take out and use in later years – whether in procession, to decorate your Sunday School space or to hang in your church. For how to make banners, see the All Saints/All Souls chapter; for bread recipes, see the Good Friday chapter.

- If you are doing this liturgy on Easter Eve, now would be a good time to take out the Alleluia banner which you made at the beginning of Lent, and decorate it, ready for it to be found on

Easter morning.

- If your congregation is open to the idea, you could use this opportunity to make and shape the bread which will be used for communion on Easter Sunday.

- If you have not done a separate Good Friday liturgy and the associated activities, many of the activities in that chapter could also be done with this one.

Here are some other ideas:

Kinaesthetic

With help from an adult leader, put together a dance to accompany one of the hymns that will be sung on Easter Sunday. If this service is taking place after Easter Sunday, you can include it in worship later in the Easter season, or replace the closing prayers and blessing of this liturgy with your dance. The dance can be as simple or complex as you like, but I've included a suggestion on pages 157–8.

Creative

- Decorating Easter eggs. Children can colour designs onto hard-boiled eggs with crayons before dipping them in the dye of their choice. This gives children the opportunity to be creative with their designs, and to incorporate some symbols and images of Holy Week and Easter. If you can find white hens' eggs, those can be used; otherwise, duck eggs work well.

- Baker Ross sells 'Scratch Art Crosses', cross-shaped decorations with a multi-coloured surface covered over with black. Children use the scratching tools (included) to scrape away the black covering and create their own brilliantly coloured design. The scraping away of darkness to reveal the light is a good metaphor for Easter, and the activity allows for creativity without requiring huge amounts of artistic skill. The decorations come with ribbons, so they can be hung in children's rooms at home, or used to decorate an 'Easter tree' in your Sunday School room or church. Baker Ross also sells 'Scratch Art Eggs'. My 5- to 11-year-olds *loved* this activity.

Multi-sensory

Hands-on storytelling materials related to the stories from the liturgy, e.g. the Exodus Storybag or the 4-in-1 Easter storytelling doll (both available from Articles of Faith), Godly Play figures, specially selected pieces from Beulah Land, etc. You can also make paper and paints available for children to respond to these storytelling materials. Along with the scent of the flowers and the taste of the cake, these provide children with a multi-sensory way of experiencing Easter.

DANCE TO 'LORD OF THE DANCE'

The dance begins with one child in the centre of the chancel and the other children in a semi-circle around the child in the centre, with the front open so the child in the centre is visible to the congregation. The child in the centre is kneeling, bent forward, head on knees. The children in the semi-circle are kneeling.

'Grapevining', as used for the movements in the final chorus, is a dance move found in many folk traditions. For 'grapevine right', dancers step to the right with their right foot. They then cross the left foot in front of the right, bending the knees. They then step right again, then cross the left foot behind the right, bending the knees, and repeat. When grapevining down an aisle, the row of dancers will necessarily be facing sideways, not facing the altar or the door.

For a good visual introduction to the grapevine step, search for 'Mayim Mayim' on YouTube. This is an Israeli folk dance that uses the basic grapevine step in a circle. It is easy to see how it could be used in a line instead.

I danced in the morning, when the world was begun. And I danced in the moon and the stars and the sun.	*Children in the semi-circle cross their arms in front of themselves at the waist, then lift them up, opening them to a round shape.* *The child in the centre (Jesus) unfolds himself and stands up in orans position.*
I came down from heaven and I danced on the earth. At Bethlehem, I had my birth.	*The children in the semi-circle stand up.* *They turn on the spot and finish by holding hands, arms still raised.*
Dance, then, wherever you may be. I am the Lord of the dance, said he, And I'll lead you all, wherever you may be, And I'll lead you all in the dance, said he.	*Jesus goes to the front of the semi-circle, his back to the congregation. He takes the hands of the two people at the ends of the semi-circle, closing the circle. Everyone in the circle walks to their left.*
I danced for the scribes and the Pharisee,	*The circle breaks, and the children who were previously in the circle form two lines, one on either side of the chancel.*
But they would not dance and they wouldn't follow me.	*Jesus faces one group, who look disapproving – wagging fingers, shaking heads, turning away, etc.*
I danced for the fishermen – for James and John. They came with me and the dance went on.	*Jesus turns to the other group, who look excited – pointing to him, nodding, etc. They all join hands. The one closest to Jesus takes his hand and they form a circle.*
Dance, then, wherever you may be. I am the Lord of the dance, said he.	*Circle right.*

| And I'll lead you all, wherever you may be, | *Circle left.* |
| And I'll lead you all in the dance, said he. | |

| I danced on the Sabbath and I cured the lame. | *Jesus drops the hands of the people in the circle and begins to place his hands on their heads, one by one.* |

| The holy people said it was a shame. They whipped and they stripped and they hung me high. | *The Pharisees surge forward. Two of them grab Jesus by his arms and move him so he is standing just in front of the altar. The rest mime whipping him.* |

| And they left me there on a cross to die. | *Jesus stretches his arms out to the sides as though on the cross. The Pharisees return to their side of the chancel, as the disciples come forward and gather around the cross.* |

| Dance, then, wherever you may be. I am the Lord of the dance, said he. And I'll lead you all, wherever you may be, And I'll lead you all in the dance, said he. | *Freeze.* |

| I danced on a Friday when the sky turned black. It's hard to dance with the devil on your back. They buried my body and they thought I'd gone. But I am the dance and I still go on! | *Two of the disciples kneel at the front of the chancel, their arms raised in front of them, fingertips touching, forming an arch. The rest of the disciples carry Jesus' body and place it in the tomb, kneeling, head bowed, on knees, as at the beginning. The disciples who are not forming the tomb form a circle around the tomb.* |

| Dance, then, wherever you may be. I am the Lord of the dance, said he. | *The disciples circle left.* |

| And I'll lead you all, wherever you may be, And I'll lead you all in the dance, said he. | *The disciples circle right.* |

| They cut me down, and I leapt up high! I am the life that will never, never die! I'll live in you if you'll live in me. I am the Lord of the dance, said he. | *The circle parts, and the two disciples forming the tomb stand. Jesus rises from kneeling, his arms raised. The Pharisees rush in and join the disciples. They all form a semi-circle, with Jesus leading, hands joined, arms raised.* |

| Dance, then, wherever you may be. I am the Lord of the dance, said he. And I'll lead you all, wherever you may be, And I'll lead you all in the dance, said he. | *Led by Jesus, the group grapevines down the centre aisle to the back of the church.* |

EXTENSIONS FOR HOME

Easter is 50 days long; therefore, I've included activities that can be done over an extended period of time. This shows children that Christ's resurrection is not confined to one day – it is a process of new life that unfolds over time, into each of our lives.

Of course every family will also have its own Easter traditions. In my family, my mother hid a dozen or so chocolate eggs around our rooms for us to find as soon as we woke up on Easter morning – besides being fun, this kept us occupied for 20 minutes or so, which gave my parents some badly needed extra sleep. There are any number of activities that can be done to decorate the house for Easter, or to help prepare the Easter table. Here, however, my aim is to provide a few activities not just for Easter *Day*, but for the Easter *season*.

Nature-related activities

The imagery of death and rebirth is reflected in the changing of the earth from winter to spring. Here are some ways to help children make these connections during the 50 days of Easter:

- *Plant bean seeds in clear plastic cups.* Press the seeds up against the edge of the cup so they are visible. Check on them every day. Talk about how you are burying the seed, just as Jesus was buried. Watch the seed split open and talk about how Jesus' body was broken and died. Ask your children, 'Is the seed dead?' Listen to their answers. Watch the green shoots move upward through the soil towards the light and talk about how this plant will grow food that will feed us. Through the death and burial of the seed, new life is given – to the plant itself and, through its fruit, to us. Just like the Resurrection and the Eucharist.

- *Buy a butterfly hatching kit* (they are available on Amazon) and send off for the larvae. Watch the caterpillars grow and make their cocoons. Talk about how they have wrapped themselves up, as Jesus was wrapped in his grave clothes. Ask your children what will happen next. When the caterpillars break out of their grave clothes, will they be the same as before, or will they have a new and wonderful kind of life? (Caterpillar and butterfly finger puppets, by the way, make excellent gifts for Easter baskets.)

- *Go on a nature walk* each week and look for signs of new life – flowers, baby animals, new leaves, etc. Keep track of what you see and how it changes. Even the most urban areas have surprising amounts of wildlife if you look closely enough.

- *Encourage your children to help you in the garden*, or tend a small plot of their own. The labour of placing bulbs and seeds in the ground, covering them up and watching them come to life will reinforce the imagery of rebirth and resurrection that is at the heart of Easter. If you don't have a garden, you can grow herbs and small flowers on a windowsill or a balcony.

PENTECOST

Come down, O love divine!

INTRODUCTION

Pentecost is an under-appreciated holiday. It is crucial in the story of the People of God – we've had the joy of Easter, the promise of new life, and Pentecost tells us, 'Now go out into the world and do something about it.' Pentecost is a challenge. It tells us we can't just sit around self-indulgently talking about how Jesus has redeemed us, personally – we have to take that Good News and use it to transform our world. The function of this liturgy is to mark that transition, through the gift of the Holy Spirit. Jesus is risen, and we have celebrated that for 50 days. Now he has ascended to heaven, but instead of leaving us alone, he has given us his Spirit. That Spirit inspires us to go forth and live out the gospel in the world.

Therefore the focus of the liturgy is on three things: reaffirming the truth of Jesus' resurrection, receiving his spirit as a dove and as fire, and going forth to tell the Good News to the world with the variety of gifts God has given each of us.

The liturgy includes a short session of 'liquid worship'. This is an alternative worship model that involves the creation of several 'stations' in the church. For a period of time, worshippers are allowed to choose which station they would like to go to, and to move freely between stations. Functionally, this is like moving some of the 'processing activities' in the other chapters from after the liturgy and placing them within it.

The four stations listed here are based on the four 'Spiritual Styles' identified by David Csinos in his book *Children's Ministry That Fits*.[1] After interviewing children about how and when they felt closest to God, he identified four predominant spiritual types that emerged. By targeting those four styles with your stations, you can enable children to choose a way of worshipping that is meaningful to them. If you have other offered talents in your congregation, you may use those.

These are the stations I suggest. Ideas for what you can do in each are provided in the 'Set-up and preparation' section of this chapter:

- symbol

- word

- action

- emotion.

Also included in the liturgy is a section when the news of the Resurrection is passed round the congregation in 'Chinese Whispers'. Using Chinese Whispers to tell the Good News of the Resurrection throughout the congregation was an idea introduced to me by the Revd Michael Fuller. Another feature of the liturgy is a section where people will read the Lord's Prayer in a range of languages.

SET-UP AND PREPARATION

For the liturgy:

1 Materials for performing the story script. This can be done in any number of ways. I use the Beulah Land feltboard set (<www.beulahenterprises.org>), but it can be acted out, told with puppets or large Godly Play figures, or in any way you can imagine. It should not, however, be made cutesy or reliant on laughs. The story has its own power – you don't need to dress it up.

2 The storyteller should begin the 'Chinese Whispers' section with the words 'Jesus Christ is Lord! He is risen from the dead and he is Lord! God's love is for everyone!'

3 At least three volunteers to read the Lord's Prayer in languages other than English. In a church, it may be difficult to find rehearsal time – you can use adults to do this part and the children can listen, and say the prayer in English, rather than participating in the multi-lingual portion themselves. It works powerfully as a merely aural experience – participation in the multi-lingual aspect of it is not necessary for it to be moving. If you struggle to find this many native speakers, see if you have a classicist among your congregation who could do it in Latin, or if the vicar is comfortable reading it in Greek. This can help you flesh out the numbers!

4 At least four liquid worship stations (see below), and volunteers to man them.

5 Music to play during liquid worship – live or recorded. This should be quiet and non-invasive. Piano music is always good; Chopin and Schubert are particularly moving and contemplative.

6 The Paschal candle, lighted.

7 Candles for every congregant, including, if you like, flameless candles for the very young (see <www.smartcandle.co.uk>).

8 As always, whenever your worship involves candles, you should have a fire extinguisher on hand.

For the liquid worship stations, I suggest:

Symbol

• the flame block set (available from Little Acorns to Mighty Oaks: <www.littleacornstomightyoaks.co.uk/shop/Wooden_toys/Grimms/Large_Fire_Stacker>);

• a group of 'disciples'. These can be made using doll's house dolls in 'hospital' robes, or you can use Godly Play figures or Playmobil figures;

• pinwheels, or other toys that require wind, or breath, to move;

• bird finger/hand puppets, or Christmas tree ornaments.

Word

This can share 'chill-out' space with the 'Emotion' station if you like (see below).

Action

• Provide materials for children to design posters inviting passers-by to come to church. Encourage children to think about what we do together and why it's important. Afterwards, laminate the posters and hang them outside the church.

- Alternatively, contact a local homelessness charity and ask if they are happy to accept donations of household goods. If they are, you can use this station as a way of starting a service project that will continue over the next few weeks or months.

  During the liquid worship session, make available red, orange and yellow paper, and a large piece of poster board (A1 or A0) or corkboard. Encourage children to make a 'flame' like the flames the signified the Spirit at Pentecost. While they are doing this, they can choose a household item they can bring in to church for the charity. They write down their name and their chosen item on the flame they have made and stick it on the poster or corkboard with Blu-Tack or a drawing pin. When they have brought in their named item, put a sticker on their flame to show they have made their donation.

  This is not a one-off activity but rather the beginning of a service project that your leaders will continue to carry out during the weeks and months following the service. Having the children 'take action' by making a promise to help others at Pentecost is a good way of kick-starting such a project and showing that Pentecost is a time when we renew our promises to do God's work in the world.

Emotion

Have a 'chill-out zone', with a rug and/or soft cushions or beanbag chairs on the floor. Create a spiritual focus in the centre – this can be anything from a table with a candle on it to a complex art installation made by children or volunteers ahead of time.

If you can, provide iPods with a variety of music on them, so children can choose to listen to something that may be different from what you have playing in the church. (Some suggestions for older children: Billy Joel's 'River of Dreams', Steeleye Span's 'Gaudete', The Beatles' 'Let it Be', 'On the Willows' from Godspell, the Byrds' 'Turn, Turn, Turn', any good recording of The Melodians' 'By the Rivers of Babylon'.)

You will need volunteers to man each station. In addition I suggest, in order to retain the feeling of sacred time and sacred space, that you have quiet music playing during the liquid worship section, and encourage volunteers to maintain a contemplative atmosphere.

If you have large groups of children, or your children are particularly boisterous, you may want to have several volunteers whose job is to 'float' around the church during the liquid worship period, maintaining order and encouraging children to choose a station.

PENTECOST LITURGY

Come down, O love divine!

COMING TOGETHER IN THE LORD'S NAME

We come into the church and sit in silence. When the service begins, we sing together, peacefully, over and over:

Ve - ni Cre - a - tor Spi - ri - tus.

Music: J. Berthier © Ateliers et Presses de Taizé, F-71250 Taizé-Communauté

Leader   Come, Creator Spirit, and fill our hearts with the fire of your love.
All   **Amen.**

Reading

From 'Whitsunday' by George Herbert

Reader   Listen sweet Dove unto my song,
            And spread thy golden wings in me;
            Hatching my tender heart so long,
            Till it get wing, and fly away with thee.

            Lord, though we change, thou art the same;
            The same sweet God of love and light:
            Restore this day, for thy great name,
            Unto his ancient and miraculous right.

Hymn

            Come down, O love divine, seek Thou this soul of mine,
            And visit it with thine own ardour glowing.
            O Comforter, draw near, within my heart appear,
            And kindle it, Thy holy flame bestowing.

            O let it freely burn, till earthly passions turn
            To dust and ashes in its heat consuming;
            And let Thy glorious light shine ever on my sight,
            And clothe me round, the while my path illuming.

            And so the yearning strong, with which the soul will long,
            Shall far outpass the power of human telling;
            For none can guess its grace, till he become the place
            Wherein the Holy Spirit makes His dwelling.

HEARING AND RESPONDING TO THE STORY

Leader   Do you remember how at Easter,
Jesus died and rose again,
with a new kind of life to share with us?
How Jesus fought death for us and won?
And do you remember how, forty days after he rose again,
Jesus went up to heaven,
to be with God his Father,
to be everywhere at once like God is?

Ten days after Jesus ascended,
his disciples – his twelve special friends – were all together in a room.
The doors were locked.
Jesus' disciples were afraid.

They were afraid of the people who had killed Jesus.

They were afraid that they would be next.

When Jesus had risen from the dead,
they had felt brave
and strong.
But now he was gone again,
up to heaven,
to be with God the Father.

And his disciples were lonely.

As they sat in the room,
suddenly there came a great wind,
rushing through the room,
and tongues of fire appeared over the heads of the disciples.

They unlocked the door and went out into the street.
They found they could speak in different languages,
to tell the good news to everyone –
men and women,
old and young,
rich and poor,
black and white,
Jews, Romans, Greeks, Persians, and everyone else,
saying,
'Jesus Christ is Lord!
He is risen from the dead and he is Lord!
God's love is for everyone!'

They found they weren't afraid any more.

It didn't matter if their enemies found them,
it didn't even matter if their enemies killed them.

Because the new life that Jesus had was in them now,
the Holy Spirit had come in wind and flame,
and made them brave and strong.

And they told others,
and those people told more people,
and through the ages and centuries, the good news has come,
until now I am telling you
and you can tell others,
men and women,
old and young,
rich and poor,
black and white.

The leader then chooses two children from the congregation and whispers something in their ears. Slowly, the good news will spread through the congregation. When you hear it, pass it on to someone near you.

The words can be found at the end of this service sheet, in case you forget them. But try not to look in advance!

Leader What is the Good News?

Everyone then says the Good News together. If you do not say it loudly and joyfully enough, the leader may make you do it again.

Leader And that's our story.

Now we get ready to say the Lord's Prayer together. We begin by saying it in English. After a few lines, somebody will stand up and begin reading it in another language. A few lines later, a third person will start reading it in a third language. This will continue until we have as many languages as possible.

Here is the prayer in English:

All **Our Father,**
Who art in heaven,
Hallowed be thy name.
Thy kingdom come.
Thy will be done on earth as it is in heaven.
Give us this day our daily bread,
And forgive us our trespasses,
As we forgive those who trespass against us.
And lead us not into temptation,
But deliver us from evil.
For thine is the kingdom, the power, and the glory,
For ever and ever. Amen.

Hymn

Refrain:
Every time I feel the spirit
Moving in my heart I will pray.
Every time I feel the spirit
Moving in my heart I will pray.

Up on the mountains my Lord spoke.
Out of His mouth came fire and smoke.
Looked all around me, it looked so fine
I asked the Lord could it be mine.

Refrain

The Jordan river is chilly and cold.
It chills the body but not the soul.
There's only one train upon this track.
It runs to heaven and then right back.

Refrain

Oh, I have sorrow and I have woe.
I have heartaches here below.
But while God leads me I'll never fear
For I know that He is near.

Refrain

LIQUID WORSHIP

During this part of the service, you have a choice about how you would like to worship.

There are different places you can go, which have different activities for learning about God and talking with him in your heart. You can move from one to another if you like.

Quiet music will play throughout this time.

When the liquid worship time is over, the leader will say:

Leader   The Lord be with you!

We all stop what we're doing and say:

All   And also with you!

We hold up anything we have made during liquid worship.

Leader   Let us pray.

Lord, in your act of creation, you showed us that you are a magnificent artist. Bless the hands that have used this time to make beautiful things, to be creative, as you are.
   In sending Jesus to live with us, you showed us that you are loving and healing. Bless the hearts that have used this time to grow close to you in prayer, silence and music.

Today, as we celebrate your gift of the Holy Spirit, we remember that you sent your Spirit upon your disciples to spur them to action, to do your will in the world. Bless those who have responded to that call today by carrying your message to others or by helping others.

Help us to remember that all our talents are gifts from you, and to use them to your praise and service. Amen.

As we return to our seats, we sing:

> Every time I feel the spirit
> Moving in my heart I will pray.
> Every time I feel the spirit
> Moving in my heart I will pray.

(Repeat until all have returned to their seats.)

BLESSING AND GOING OUT

The leader lights his or her candle from the Paschal candle, and then lights the candle of one person in the congregation. We share the light among us, from one person to the next, until all of us are holding some of the light.

Leader   At Pentecost, the Spirit of God came in wind and fire. Grant that as we go out into the world, that fire of God may burn still in our hearts, and God's love surround us like the wind.

All   **Amen!**

Hymn

> Give me oil in my lamp, keep me burning.
> Give me oil in my lamp, I pray.
> Give me oil in my lamp, keep me burning.
> Keep me burning 'til the break of day.
>
> > *Refrain:*
> > *Sing hosanna, sing hosanna,*
> > *Sing hosanna to the King of Kings!*
> > *Sing hosanna, sing hosanna,*
> > *Sing hosanna to the King!*
>
> Give me joy in my heart, keep me praising.
> Give me joy in my heart, I pray.
> Give me joy in my heart, keep me praising.
> Keep me praising 'til the break of day.
>
> > *Refrain*
>
> Give me peace in my heart, keep me resting.
> Give me peace in my heart, I pray.
> Give me peace in my heart, keep me resting.
> Keep me resting 'til the break of day.
>
> > *Refrain*

Give me love in my heart, keep me serving.
Give me love in my heart, I pray.
Give me love in my heart, keep me serving.
Keep me serving 'til the break of day.

Refrain

These are the words the leader whispers at the end of the story:

'Jesus Christ is Lord!
He is risen from the dead and he is Lord!
God's love is for everyone!'

ADDING A EUCHARIST

The Eucharist in this liturgy could take place directly after the liquid worship section. Anything that was made during liquid worship could be brought to the altar as an offertory along with the elements, and, along with the non-tangible worship offered during liquid worship, blessed by the priest.

If you want to add an offertory hymn while this was happening, I'd suggest 'Here I Am, Lord'. It's appropriate for Pentecost, with its theme of mission and service.

ADAPTATIONS FOR SCHOOLS

This liturgy can be easily done in schools by including a series of 'wondering' questions, à la Godly Play (see Introduction), in place of the liquid worship section. Here are some you could use:

'I wonder what your favourite part of the story was.'
'I wonder what the most important part of the story was.'
'I wonder if you could take out anything and still have all the story you need.'
'I wonder what it would feel like to have the Holy Spirit come into your life.'
'I wonder how the disciples suddenly knew the different languages.'
'I wonder if you have any questions about the story.'

If you'd still like to include the idea of liquid worship, you can set up liquid worship stations in the assembly space later in the day, and one class at a time can come in and explore them. Create a 'sacred space' using meditative music and decorations, and dim the lights. You could begin by bringing the children into the centre of the space and praying in silence for a minute or two, before allowing them to move around the stations.

For the reading of the Lord's Prayer in various languages, you can use pupils who may have a different home language, and a short rehearsal will be all that's needed.

If your school is too large for every child to have a candle in the closing session, the child at the end of each row could hold a candle. This would still allow you to spread the light through the whole space, from front to back. Just ensure you have sensible children at the end of each row! Or, as suggested in previous chapters, invest in enough flameless candles for everyone to have one, and invite them to turn them on one class at a time, spreading the light throughout the space.

EXTENSION ACTIVITIES

The imagery of this festival is simple – the wind, the fire and the dove. Alongside that is the theme of speaking the gospel in every language, to all people. It is a feast of mission, of inclusion, of God's goodness to us in his gift of the Spirit. It is a festival that teaches us that we are not alone, because God's spirit is in us, and we cannot be complacent, because God has chosen us to do his work in the world.

Also, importantly, Pentecost usually arrives at a fairly convenient time. Unlike Christmas and Easter, it doesn't take place over school holidays (unless it happens to coincide with half-term), and there is a seven-week gap between Easter and Pentecost that can allow you to take some time to prepare children for the festival at a time when you're not consumed with the craziness of Holy Week or the run-up to Christmas.

Preparation activities

Candle decorating

Detailed information about candle decorating can be found in the list of processing activities in the Christmas chapter. The children can make or decorate candles which can be used as the light is shared through the congregation at the end of the liturgy.

Pentecost windsocks

Children decorate a coloured piece of A3 paper (I suggest using red, orange or yellow – the colours of flames). You then attach streamers to one of the long sides of the paper, and staple the short sides together into a tube. Using a hole-punch, make two holes in the top and string a ribbon through them. Hang the windsocks above the congregation during the service, so children can see the wind moving all around them. After the service, children can take them home, as a sign of the presence of the Spirit in their lives.

Mobiles

You can make mobiles to hang over the congregation by tying two dowels together at right angles, tying ribbon to all four ends, and tying the ribbons together over the middle. Children can make doves and flames to hang from the mobile, which can then be hung over the congregation (see Figure 11). Gertrud Mueller Nelson goes into more detail about this idea in her book, *To Dance With God: Family ritual and community celebration*.[2]

Planning mission opportunities

With guidance from their leaders, children can think of ways to carry the Church's mission into the world. I would be wary of allowing this to turn into an event where children are explicitly told to evangelize to others. I believe this co-opts children for an adult agenda in a way that is unacceptable.

Here are some ideas for ways in which children can bear witness to their faith in the wider world:

• *Design a T-shirt* with a religious message on it, which can then be made and given to the children. They can be encouraged to wear the shirt to the Pentecost service and take it home with them, to wear whenever they like. Children could agree on a design, and then each draw a different part of it, or you could have a competition, with the winning design made into a shirt and all the designs displayed in the church somewhere.

Figure 11 *Mobile by Serena Janssens, age ten*

- *Choose something they've learned about* in Sunday School and plan a way to present their learning to the wider church. They could perform a play in place of a lesson during a service one week, telling the story of that lesson. They could put together a presentation about a Gospel story and present it in place of the sermon. They could practise and sing a piece of music as an anthem during a service. They could host a stall at a church fete or a community event, telling people about children's programmes at your church. The purpose is to give children an opportunity to talk about their faith to a receptive audience, rather than sending them out to 'make converts'. By sharing their faith with the rest of the church community, or with people who voluntarily stop by a stall, they are given a chance to do this.

Storyboarding

The storytelling during the liturgy is detailed, and provides a context for linking Pentecost back to Easter; if you want to reinforce this, here's an activity that will help put Pentecost in its biblical context.

Hollywood directors do something called 'storyboarding', where they make pictures of what every shot in their film will look like. Starting with Easter, make a storyboard of each post-Resurrection appearance – the empty tomb, Jesus' appearance in the locked room, the Road to Emmaus, Doubting Thomas, breakfast on the shore of the lake, and the Ascension. These can then be placed along the route people will walk coming into the Pentecost liturgy, so they can see 'the story so far' as they come in. More information on making storyboards, and some examples, can be found at <accad.osu.edu/womenandtech/Storyboard%20Resource>.

If you prefer, you could illustrate the story as a comic strip. This is more polished than a storyboard, and includes narration and dialogue rather than just a sketch of the different parts of each scene, with a description underneath it explaining what's going on.

Processing activities

Pentecost celebrates the Christian mission. You can follow up your Pentecost liturgy by carrying out the mission activities you planned in the lead-up to it, but it's difficult to do those immediately after the liturgy, in the format of a Family Day. So here are a few ways to translate mission into action immediately after the liturgy:

Pavement evangelism

Hand out thick outdoor chalks to each child and set them loose, drawing on the pavement outside the church, with 'pictures from today's service and story' as a guideline. You could brainstorm ideas beforehand – dove, flame, altar, groups of people, the words 'God's love is for everyone', the Risen Jesus, etc. The pictures will soon be washed away by the rain, but in the meantime, passers-by will see your church's mission literally spilling out of its front door and into the street.

In rural parishes that may not have pavements outside, you could prepare signs on wooden poles in advance. Children can decorate them and then you can stick them in the ground leading from your church down the path to the road.

Balloon release

Each child has a piece of paper with the church's logo on it and a big blank space. Children decorate the paper with images from the liturgy or from a Bible story of their choosing. The papers are then stapled to the ribbon of a helium balloon. When everyone is done, the group goes outside and releases their balloons. (If you like, you can include the church's email address/ Twitter name/Facebook page address on the paper and ask whoever finds the balloon to 'check in' and tell you where it landed.)

Please note that you should use biodegradable balloons and biodegradable ribbons for this activity, so you are not damaging the environment.

Pray one for me

The website <www.prayoneforme.org> allows anyone to submit a prayer, under a range of categories, and the prayer team responsible for the site will include your submissions in their prayers. Have a table with a few laptops on it, and with the website open on them. Children can pray along with the prayers of others, or offer their own prayer, creating a link between the liturgy they have just experienced and the broader church.

A Pentecost party

Pentecost is also a festival celebrating Christian community – the apostles are transformed by the gift of the Spirit and become the Church. You could finish with a Pentecost party to celebrate your community of apostles.

Decorations

As I mentioned before, the themes of wind, fire, doves and different languages are the main sources of Pentecost imagery.

If you have decorated the church with windsocks and/or mobiles, you could hold some back to decorate your party space, extending the 'presence' of the Holy Spirit out of the church itself and into the world. Alternatively, bunches of red, orange and yellow helium balloons will create a flame-like effect (and could be used in a balloon release at the end of the party – see notes above on making these environmentally responsible).

Hang Christmas tree dove ornaments from the tables or from light fixtures in the ceiling, and string 'flags of the world' bunting around your space to reinforce the idea of different languages and nations receiving the word of God.

Sprinkle dove-shaped confetti over your tables (yes, it exists – you can find it on eBay and wedding supply companies) and light lots of candles (or flameless candles, for a safer option).

To combine the two images of doves and flames, you can use the fabulous paper lanterns with dove designs from Party Delights (<partydelights.co.uk> – search for 'white dove candle bags'). If you'd like to make your own, instructions for making paper lanterns can be found in the Christmas chapter.

Food

Again, reinforcing the global focus of Pentecost, you could have a buffet of international food at your party. If you are lucky enough to have an international congregation, with active volunteers, you can even have the congregation supply the food.

Entertainment

Putumayo World Music makes a *Kids World Party* CD, which is available on Amazon. It includes party songs for children from cultures around the world. They also have a series of *Playground* CDs, from *European Playground* to *Caribbean Playground*, which feature upbeat songs from different parts of the world.

These could be used as background music during the party, and also for games such as Musical Chairs or Musical Statues.

Here are some more games with a Pentecost theme:

Opposites

This is a drama game that is infinitely adaptable and can be used with almost any story. It's best for Key Stage 1 children (ages 5 to 7). You start by asking children to identify the feelings the apostles had in the Pentecost story, before and after the Spirit came. Some variation of 'scared' and 'brave' will come up. Ask children to come up with a way of moving that stands for 'scared' and one that stands for 'brave'. Choose the easiest or the best one, and teach it to the group, then get them to practise moving around the party space as you shout 'Scared!' or 'Brave!' at irregular intervals. Then add another pair of words – 'wind' and 'fire'. Ask them to come up with movements for that, and add 'wind' and 'fire' to the repertoire of words you call out randomly.

Once they've got the hang of this, you mix it up a bit – whatever you call out, they have to do the movement that goes with its opposite. For example, if you call out 'Brave', they have to do the movement for 'scared', and vice versa. If people start doing the one you call out, instead of its opposite, they are 'out'. You can keep going until you have one winner, but very often you'll have five or six who are good enough not to get caught out, so you may want to call time once you hit that point.

Pass the Parcel

You can adapt this game for Pentecost by putting 'gifts' related to the Holy Spirit inside the parcel. The seven gifts of the spirit are very abstract, so it's difficult to make gifts specifically for those, but you could include a candle-decorating kit (flames) a dove-shaped Christmas tree ornament, a bird finger puppet, a small pinwheel (wind), mini wind chimes, and so on.

Chinese Whispers

Your children will have already done this in the liturgy, but the goal there was to keep the message intact. Here you can be a bit sillier and see how the message gets changed over time. (With older children, you could bring this up at a youth group meeting later and talk about how this can affect our reading of the Bible – it's at the end of an oral tradition and perhaps there are parts of it that have changed from the original. How can we read it knowing that it is both the work of a perfect God and of imperfect humans?)

Choose someone to be the 'Holy Spirit' and start the message, and go all around the circle, seeing how it changes by the end. If you'd like to keep your messages sacred, rather than letting the children choose what to say, you can have a bowl full of Bible verses on folded paper, and the children can choose one from the bowl instead of coming up with their own ideas. You need to be confident enough in your children's respect for the Bible that it can withstand a little oral-tradition mangling from the game.

Here are some suggestions:

Exodus 31.3: 'I have filled my servant with the Spirit of God, with ability and intelligence.'

2 Samuel 23.2: 'The Spirit of the LORD speaks by me, his word is upon my tongue.'

Psalm 51.11: 'Cast me not away from your presence, and take not your holy Spirit from me.'

Isaiah 11.2: 'The Spirit of the LORD shall rest on him, the spirit of wisdom and understanding, the spirit of counsel and might, the spirit of knowledge and the fear of the LORD.'

Isaiah 44.3: 'For I will pour water on the thirsty land, and streams on the dry ground; I will pour my Spirit upon your descendants, and my blessing on your offspring.'

Isaiah 61.1: 'The Spirit of the Lord GOD is upon me, because the LORD has anointed me to bring good news to the poor.'

Ezekiel 11.19: 'And I will give them one heart, and put a new spirit within them; I will take the stony heart out of their flesh and give them a heart of flesh.'

Ezekiel 43.5: 'The Spirit lifted me up, and brought me into the inner court; and behold, the glory of the LORD filled the temple.'

Joel 2.28: 'I will pour out my spirit on all flesh; your sons and your daughters shall prophesy, your old men shall dream dreams, and your young men shall see visions.'

Haggai 2.5b: 'My Spirit abides among you; fear not.'

Wisdom 12.1: 'Your immortal spirit is in all things.'

Matthew 3.11: 'He will baptize you with the Holy Spirit and with fire.'

Matthew 12.18: 'Behold, my servant whom I have chosen, my beloved with whom my soul is well pleased. I will put my Spirit upon him, and he shall proclaim justice.'

Matthew 28.19: 'Go therefore and make disciples of all nations, baptizing them in the name of the Father and of the Son and of the Holy Spirit.'

John 3.8: 'The wind blows where it wills, and you hear the sound of it, but you do not know where it comes from or where it goes; so it is with everyone who is born of the Spirit.'

John 14.26: 'But the Counsellor, the Holy Spirit, whom the Father will send in my name, he will teach you all things.'

John 16.13: 'When the Spirit of truth comes, he will guide you into all the truth.'

Acts 2.4: 'They were all filled with the Holy Spirit and began to speak in other tongues.'

Romans 8.14: 'All who are led by the Spirit of God are children of God.'

1 Corinthians 12.4: 'There are varieties of gifts, but the same Spirit.'

Favours

At the church I grew up in, we had an Epiphany party – at the end of this, cardboard stars covered with metallic paper were given out to everyone as a favour. On each star was a printed label with a Bible verse about light. I pinned mine to the corkboard in my bedroom and soon had a collection of Bible verses hanging above my desk without even trying. You can do this at Pentecost with dove decorations.

Wedding place cards often have doves on them, or are cut in the shape of doves, and can be bought fairly reasonably. <Etsy.com> has an amazing selection – just type 'dove place cards' into the search field. Alternatively, you can search eBay for dove-themed place cards or decorations.

This can be a great way of reminding children that the Spirit of God is with them as they go out from church into the world – and if they hang the card up in their room, the verse, and the imagery of the dove, will become more familiar to them.

EXTENSIONS FOR HOME

Charity projects

With its message of taking the message of Christ out into the world, Pentecost is a good time to get your children involved in charitable projects. The weather is (theoretically) good, so there are lots of sponsored walks at this time of year – sit down with your children and talk about what Jesus was like, what he did, the sort of people he helped, and what charities they might have heard of who are helping those same kinds of people.

- Jesus healed the sick – get your children involved in one of the myriad walks for cancer research held around the country.

- He showed concern for children – see if the NSPCC has ways of getting involved in your area.

- He commanded us to care for the poor and needy – talk to your children about Oxfam's work and clear out any unused items from your house to take to your local Oxfam shop (don't pressure your children to get rid of things, though – this may teach them to resent giving to charity, if it is forced upon them).

- He condemned those who trampled the oppressed, so talk to your children about Fairtrade and see what household goods you could be ordering from Traidcraft instead of buying them from the supermarket. When you do go to the supermarket, encourage your children to seek out items with the Fairtrade logo on them.

If there are places where your children could become actively involved, e.g. serving dinner at a homeless shelter (with you, of course, not on their own), Pentecost is a good time to explore them. We are Jesus' hands and heart in the world – the Spirit is within us now.

Gifts mobile

Similar to making mobiles at church, as detailed in the 'Preparation activities' section, but with a twist. For this mobile, your family will make one dove to represent each member of the family. You can include extended family if you like – it doesn't have to only be the people who live in your house.

Start by reading 1 Corinthians 12.1–11 (or 1–22 if your children have longer attention spans). Pray together for God to help you see all the gifts he has given the people in your family.

On each dove, write the name of the person it represents, and the gifts the Spirit has given that person. Don't forget to include personal qualities, such as kindness, compassion, helpfulness, thoughtfulness, curiosity and so on, as well as more visible talents like singing, being in the top group for maths, or being a great footballer. Consider that the same trait you struggle with in your child may actually be a gift – the child who is shy, whose social life you worry over, may have the gift of being able to be happy enjoying quiet times alone with God. The shy child's sibling, who you worry is a show-off, might have the gift of leadership and the ability to inspire others. Allow children to name each other's gifts, and yours, as well as their own.

When the mobile is finished, hang it in a communal space, as a reminder that your family is blessed with unique gifts of the Spirit. Bless the mobile and pray together that you will use your gifts in the way God wants you to.

READING LIST AND WEB RESOURCES FOR WORSHIP WITH CHILDREN

This list is not intended to be exhaustive. Rather, it is a selection of resources for inspiration in doing liturgy with children.

Theory and pedagogy

Bruno Bettelheim, *The Uses of Enchantment: The meaning and importance of fairy tales* (New York: Alfred A. Knopf, 1976; London: Penguin, 1991)

This book was a breakthrough in understanding children's development and has obvious applications to spirituality and religious development. Bettelheim is a psychoanalyst who argues that fairy tales have powerful symbolic meaning to the struggles of our own lives, and that allowing children to work through them and gain mastery over them was crucial in their development. Analysing classic fairy tales such as 'Little Red Riding Hood' one by one, he gives children's workers, clergy and teachers plenty of food for thought on how we present the archetypally rich stories of the Bible to our children.

David M. Csinos, *Children's Ministry That Fits: Beyond one-size-fits-all approaches to nurturing children's spirituality*, with a foreword by Brian D. McLaren and an afterward by Joyce E. Bellous (Eugene, OR: Wipf & Stock, 2011)

Based on children's own reports of their four different ways of knowing God – emotion, action, word and symbol – this book is a good resource on how to avoid a 'one size fits all' approach in our ministry.

Gerard Jones, *Killing Monsters: Why children need fantasy, super heroes, and make-believe violence* (New York: Basic Books, 2003)

While Jones is primarily concerned with popular culture rather than religion and spirituality, this book has obvious connections to children's spirituality. Many of the stories in the Bible include violence and danger, and children's workers often feel the urge to remove the sad or scary parts. Jones argues – and I quote him extensively on the topic in the All Saints chapter – that this can be damaging to children. Using empirical research, case studies and interviews, he puts together a clear and cogent argument for why make-believe violence can be not only acceptable but actually healthy.

Dr Rebecca Nye, *Children's Spirituality: What it is and why it matters* (London: Church House Publishing, 2009)

Rebecca Nye is well known in the fields of Christian education and children's spirituality, and this book should be on every children's worker's shelf. Nye argues that spirituality is an innate part of childhood, something children are born with. Our task, therefore, is to encourage the development of something that is already there, not to fill an empty pitcher with something external. She points out how well-meaning churches can often actually be harming children's spiritual development, and presents clear practical suggestions for how to change this.

Rob Parsons, *Getting Your Kids Through Church Without Them Ending Up Hating God* (Oxford: Lion Hudson, 2011)

This book is very accessible, and an easy read. Parsons discusses the needs of children at different ages, based on Westerhoff's model of faith development, and encourages us to welcome children and young people as they are, not as who we want them to be. The concerns he addresses may be more relevant in Evangelical or Baptist churches than in mainstream Church of England churches, but the book is still worth a read, as any church is probably guilty of at least one of the 'Big Five' killers of faith that Parsons mentions.

Gretchen Wolff Pritchard, *Offering the Gospel to Children* (Cambridge, MA: Cowley Press, 1992)

Gretchen Wolff Pritchard is an American author with over 30 years' experience in parish ministry. The first half of the book is a passionate, articulate defence of Christian education that takes children and Christianity seriously and does not talk down to children or offer them a weak, graceless 'kiddie gospel', while the second is a series of essays giving practical advice on how to do this effectively. In the interests of full disclosure, I should mention that Pritchard is my mother, and several of the ideas in *Offering the Gospel to Children* have been adapted, with her permission, into the liturgies and celebrations of this book.

Margaret Withers, *Mission-Shaped Children* (London: Church House Publishing, 2006)

This is based on the principles of 'Mission-Shaped Church' and includes case studies and ideas for bringing worship experiences to children outside Sunday morning, as well as ideas for how to be the church for the entire community.

Worship resources

Gillian Ambrose, Peter Craig-Wild, Diane Craven and Mary Hawes, *Together for a Season* (London: Church House Publishing, 2006)

This series of three books takes churches through the Christian year, and includes All-Age Eucharists for important feast days, creative suggestions for making worship multi-sensory, and additional material for use at home and in church.

Elizabeth F. Caldwell, *Making a Home for Faith* (Cleveland, OH: Pilgrim Press, revised edition 2007)

Based on the thesis that faith is passed down to children through story and ritual, Caldwell provides a thoughtful framework for parents to consider their own faith and how to transmit it to their children through family life.

Dermot Donnelly, Gerard Conroy, Daughters of St Paul and MaryLouise Winters, *How to Survive the Rest of Your Life: A practical user's guide* (Boston, MA: Pauline Books and Media, 2006)

A good source of prayers for worship with teenagers and young people. Includes prayers for rites of passage such as exams, as well as for daily life. It also makes a good confirmation gift.

Gertrud Mueller Nelson, *To Dance With God: Family ritual and community celebration* (New York: Paulist Press, 1986)

This fantastic book includes ideas for family and communal celebration through the seasons of the year, along with insightful commentary.

St Gregory of Nyssa Episcopal Church (<www.saintgregorys.org/worship/resources>)

This church, in San Francisco, California, has been at the forefront of developing innovative yet traditional worship for 30 years. Influenced by the Orthodox and Catholic traditions as well as the heritage of the Anglican Communion, its services are vibrant without being tacky, interactive without being twee. While these resources are not designed specifically for children, they are an excellent starting point for All-Age Worship, and include many ideas that can be adapted for worship with children.

Worship Workshop (<www.worshipworkshop.org.uk>)

This easy, user-friendly website put together by the Revd Mary Hawes, National Advisor on Children's Ministries, is a terrific resource for developing your own liturgies with children. A standard template is provided and the website takes you step by step through the process of liturgical planning, with suggestions of themes, hymns, prayers and resources to guide you along the way. The glossary is comprehensive and clearly explained – it can be used on its own in Sunday School lessons to help develop children's liturgical vocabulary. There is also an extensive music library, which can be used both for teaching hymns and for celebrations.

REFERENCES

Harvest Festival

1 The Revd Grace Pritchard Burson, unpublished paper for M. Div. degree at Yale Divinity School.

2 Available at <www.churchofengland.org/prayer-worship/worship/texts/additional-eucharistic-prayers.aspx>.

All Saints/All Souls

1 Suzanne Collins, *The Hunger Games* (London: Scholastic, 2009).

2 Stephenie Meyer, *Twilight* (London: Atom, 2006).

3 Bruno Bettelheim, *The Uses of Enchantment: The meaning and importance of fairy tales* (London: Penguin, 1991).

4 Gerard Jones, *Killing Monsters: Why children need fantasy, super heroes, and make-believe violence* (New York: Basic Books, 2003), pp. 65–6.

5 Jones, *Killing Monsters*, p. 67.

6 Jones, *Killing Monsters*, p. 67.

7 Gretchen Wolff Pritchard, editorial page accompanying the Fall 2 edition of *The Sunday Paper*, 2009.

Christmas

1 Gertrud Mueller Nelson, *To Dance With God: Family ritual and community celebration* (New York: Paulist Press, 1986).

2 Tomie de Paola, *The Night of Las Posadas* (London: Puffin Books, 2001).

Epiphany

1 Jeanette Winter, *Follow the Drinking Gourd* (New York: Dragonfly Books, 1992).

2 Various Artists, *Christmas Around the World* (Putumayo Presents, 2003).

Ash Wednesday

1 Richard Chartres, *Tree of Knowledge, Tree of Life* (London: Continuum 2005).

Good Friday

1 Gretchen Wolff Pritchard, *Risen With Christ* (New Haven, CT: The Sunday Paper, 1988).

2 Angela Elwell Hunt and Tim Jonke, *The Tale of Three Trees* (Oxford: Lion Hudson, 2009).

3 Patricia Polacco, *Chicken Sunday* (New York: Philomel, 1992).

4 Tomie de Paola, *Nana Upstairs and Nana Downstairs* (London: Puffin, 2000).

5 Jerome W. Berryman, *Godly Play*, Volume 4 (Denver, CO: Living the Good News, 2002).

Pentecost

1 David M. Csinos, *Children's Ministry That Fits: Beyond one-size-fits-all approaches to nurturing children's spirituality* (Eugene, OR: Wipf & Stock, 2011).

2 Gertrud Mueller Nelson, *To Dance With God: Family ritual and community celebration* (New York: Paulist Press, 1986).